PRESS PAUSE
. . . PRESS ON

*Bringing Balance & Perspective
To Work & Life*

BY PATRICIA KATZ

PRESS PAUSE . . . PRESS ON
By Patricia Katz

Second Printing – October, 2010

Copyright © 2006 – Patricia Katz, Optimus Consulting
315 O'Brien Place
Saskatoon, Saskatchewan
Canada S7K 6S9
www.patkatz.com / www.pauseworks.com

All rights reserved.
No part of this book may be reproduced, transmitted or used in any form without written
permission of the publisher, except by a reviewer,
who may quote brief passages in a review.

Library and Archives Canada Cataloguing in Publication

Katz, Patricia
      Press pause... press on : bringing balance & perspective to work & life / by Patricia Katz.

Includes bibliographical references.
ISBN 978-0-9734087-1-3

      1. Quality of life.   2. Time management.   3. Self-actualization
(Psychology)   I. Title.

BF637.S4K355 2006   158.1   C2006-903751-5

Design Layout & Illustrations by:
Brian Kachur, BVK Creations – www.bvkcreations.ca

Edited by:
Barbara McNichol, Barbara McNichol Editorial – www.barbaramcnichol.com

Author Photograph by:
Stuart Kasdorf, Kasdorf Photographics – www.stuartkasdorf.com

Printed and Bound in Canada by:
Houghton Boston Printers & Lithographers – www.houghtonboston.com

Praise For Pause

"Thought provoking."

•

"A breath of fresh air."

•

"Sane and solid advice."

•

"Timeless nuggets of wisdom."

•

"Great for gaining perspective."

•

"Refreshing, encouraging, soulful."

•

"A calming influence in a crazy world."

Acknowledgments

As Press Pause ... Press On goes to press, I'm grateful to so many people in so many ways.

Thanks to my husband, David, an analyst with the soul of a poet. I value your sharp mind, your loving heart, and your boundless support. Everybody needs someone like you on side.

Thanks to my daughters, Tristan and Lindsay, for giving me two very compelling reasons to step back from the busyness. Your presence brings meaning to my life.

Thanks to my parents, Ruth and Norman, for raising me on a prairie farm with its ready access to nature's quiet places to pause and let the world go by. Your gifts travel with me.

Thanks to my five sisters (Bobbi, Shelley, Peggy, Sandra, and Susan) for teaching me the joy of relationship. You will always matter in my life.

Thanks to Lillas and Linda, my Balance Days buddies, for a decade of quarterly time-outs. Our hard-won learnings about balance and renewal have made a world of difference in my life.

Thanks to my many colleagues and clients for your confidence in my abilities and for 20 years of opportunities to be of service. You challenge me daily.

Thanks to the many readers of my weekly e-zine, Pause, for sharing your thoughts and experiences with me. Your generosity enriches the pages of this book.

Special thanks to my two collaborators on this project. It was a joy to work with both of you.

- Barbara McNichol (www.barbaramcnichol.com) brought her superb editing skills to bear on the text. What you are about to read is much stronger because of her magic way with words.
- Brian Kachur (www.bvkcreations.ca) is a brilliant illustrator who translates ideas into images with skill and ease. His lively interpretations breathe life into every concept.

And, finally, thanks to you, the reader, for pausing to dip into the pages of this book. Together, we can build a more appreciative world in our workplaces and our homes - one thoughtful reflection and one purposeful action at a time.

Other Titles By Patricia Katz

Booklets:

Give Me A Break – 67 Ways To Pause When You Absolutely Positively Do Not Have The Time

E Books:

Boost – A 7 Day Renewal Sampler

PEP – Pause Enhances Performance – A 31 Day Renewal Program

Balance Days – Guide & Journal *(with L. Hatala & L. McCann)*

Print Books:

Expert Women Who Speak ... Speak Out *(Anthology Contributor)*

WorkTips – Organizing Strategies For A Productive Worklife

HomeTips – Organizing Strategies For A Streamlined Homelife

Getting It Together – How To Organize Your Work, Your Home, and Yourself

Available at www.patkatz.com & www.pauseworks.com

About The Author

On the second printing of this book, I find myself approaching my 25th year in business as a writer and speaker. Today, I work as a Productivity & Balance Strategist, helping leaders and teams reduce the impact of overload in their lives and workplaces. My objectives are stronger results and a more satisfying work and life experience for all.

The early years of my business were devoted exclusively to questions of efficiency – being organized, using time well, getting things done. I came to realize that many highly productive individuals continued to feel pressed for time, overwhelmed by their workloads, and disappointed with their accomplishments. I began to investigate – through research and Masters-level study – the concept of time starvation. That led to my focus on helping both individuals and organizations restore the rhythm of renewal to work and life, to balance the "press for performance" with an equally important "pause for renewal."

On my websites (www.pauseworks.com and www.patkatz.com) you will find many helpful articles, surveys, and references on issues of life balance, renewal, time and stress management. You will also find suggestions for how my speaking, training and consulting services can help you and your organization accomplish what matters most in ways that bring more peace of mind.

The websites profile my credentials as an educator, communicator, media resource, innovator, contributor, and life-long learner. But mostly I prefer to be known for giving people full permission to create lives that are graceful, relaxed, healthy, productive, purposeful, focused, profitable, connected, thoughtful, appreciative, and calm! Those are my wishes for you.

> Press pause...think again,
> Patricia Katz
> info@patkatz.com

Table Of Contents

Introduction 1

Chapter One - Time Out
    Permission to Pause 3
    You'll Never Be Done Again 5
    Enough Already 7
    White Space 9
    Pull The Plug 11
    MOKALECH 13
    Vital Vacations 15
    Breathing 17

Chapter Two – Speed Traps
    Artificial Urgency 19
    Badges of Honor 21
    Cruise Control 23
    Less Flap ... More Focus 25
    Busyness 27
    Pace Setting 29
    Raging Bull 31
    Stop-Sign Buddies 33

Chapter Three – Pause Practices
    Courage 35
    Lingering 37
    Magnanimity 39
    Margins 41
    Presence 43
    Surrendering 45
    "Unitasking" 47
    Wabi Sabi 49

Chapter Four – Shifting Strategies
    Focus Time 51
    Lock-On Listening 53
    Pep Breaks 55
    Targets 57
    Rituals 59
    Sanity Policies 61
    "Simplicizing" 63
    Plimsoll Line 65

Chapter Five – Subtle Distinctions
    Empty or Full? 67
    Giving Up or Letting Go? 69
    Hurting or Healing? 71
    "One Of" or Repeat? 73
    Racing or Dancing? 75
    Mired or Motivated 77
    Save or Savor? 79
    Yes, No, or Middle Ground? 81

Chapter Six – Getting Unstuck
    Answers Are Inside 83
    In What Order? 85
    Move 'Em Out ... Move On 87
    Press Pause ... Press On 89
    Speak Up 91
    Shift Your Intentions 93
    "Unwhelm" Yourself 95
    Zap a Snit 97

Chapter Seven – Positive Mindsets
    Exercise Your Options 99
    Ask The Good-News Question 101
    It Is What It Is 103
    Give to Live 105
    Move Things Forward 107
    Reset Your Mindset 109
    Celebrate Yourself 111
    We Are They 113

Chapter Eight – Powerful Perspectives
    Be Here Now 115
    Comes With The Territory 117
    Dive Deep 119
    Find Hidden Value 121
    In Lieu of Flowers 123
    Lift Up Your Eyes 125
    Bless The Stress 127
    What Next? 129

  Endnotes 131

  Books ... And More Books 132

Introduction

Skyrocketing expectations and accelerated speed drive many of us around the bend and out of control. Recurring cycles of crash and burn take a huge toll on our health, wellness, and productivity. The numbing daily experience of blur and endure flat-out demoralizes us.

When we stretch ... and stretch ... and stretch ... without relief ... we snap! The astounding human and organizational costs of exhaustion, absenteeism, depression, and declining performance continue to soar.

All this is neither news nor a surprise. What is news is that the first line of defense against this dis-ease is a remedy that's so simple and readily available: Giving ourselves and each other Permission to Pause.

The concept is simple, but I promise you it won't be easy.

> "Slow down and everything you are chasing will come around and catch you."
> – John de Paola

Pausing begins with a shift in mindset that permits a shift of habits. At its root is an invitation to challenge the "don't stop till you drop" imperative - to instead become more thoughtful, reflective, and appreciative in the face of the nonstop pressures of a hurried world. It's a decision you make that it's okay to stop - if just for a moment. In fact, pausing is essential. Our workloads are often so full that even if we ran nonstop for the rest of our lives, we would never be done again.

In the pursuit of further and faster, we've discarded the habit of renewal. Sure, we're great at "pressing for performance." But the art of "pausing for renewal" is buried deep under a mountain of lists and schedules ... and the technology that supports it all.

Individuals, relationships, and organizations can't be sustained without embracing the habits of rejuvenation and renewal. Endless exhaustion is not an option.

Taking momentary pauses in our busy days creates opportunities (both as individuals and as organizations) to:
- Refresh our perspective
- Realign our values
- Rediscover our purpose
- Recall our intentions
- Refocus our priorities
- Reframe our problems
- Rethink our options
- Reconnect our relationships
- Refuel our bodies
- Rebuild our capacity
- Reclaim delight

It's only by pressing the pause button in our lives that we can restore balance, productivity, and perspective to life and work.

This book features a collection of 64 concepts, prompts, and word cues designed to reinforce your best practices, challenge your thinking, and, where necessary, reset your mindset. It's based on my weekly e-zine, Pause, A Voice of Sanity in a Speed-Crazed World, read by thousands of subscribers worldwide.

As I've put my ideas out there, readers have responded. Each concept presented here is supplemented by real-life experiences that Pause readers have shared. You'll be inspired by their stories and reassured to learn that you aren't alone.

It's time to give ourselves and each other permission to balance the "press for performance" with a "pause for renewal" - and restore that natural rhythm of renewal to work and life.

Welcome to the world of renewal. Press pause ... press on.

Warmly,

Patricia

Permission to Pause

You're climbing a mountain. It's a tough, dirty, exhausting challenge. You finally reach the summit only to find a higher peak beyond it. That peak makes the first one look tiny in comparison. You scramble back down and immediately set out in the direction of the bigger challenge on the horizon.

When someone asks about the view from the top, you have to admit that you never noticed. When someone asks about the experience, you note how disappointed you are that you haven't yet reached the highest point of land.

Do you recognize any patterns here? Does your life sometimes feel like one demanding mountain trek after another? If so, you could be missing the depth of experience, the satisfaction of progress, and the opportunity to learn along the way. Life without pause can be one big, hollow, empty echo. One footstep ... then another ... and another ... and another.

> "People who cannot find time for recreation are obliged, sooner or later, to find time for illness."
>
> – John Wanamaker

Pauses come in all shapes and sizes. A two-minute break in the midst of a task. A short walk at lunch. An afternoon of do-nothing puttering. A long weekend at the cabin. A three-week vacation in the mountains. A six-month sabbatical.

What do pauses have in common? A break in the action. A change of pace. A change of focus. A distance from the commotion of the moment. An opportunity for improved wellness, wisdom, and productivity.

To develop the habit of pause, start small. In the midst of a frenzied day, give yourself permission to pause. Step back. Take a moment. Take your pulse. Take a breath. Take a look. Tune in to yourself and tune in to your surroundings. It's a small first step in a deeply satisfying direction.

I came down with a cold and decided to take time off work to rest. Normally, I would work until I dropped. I rested and the world didn't cease spinning. There were clothes to wash, dishes in the sink, dogs to walk, and email messages to answer. Instead, I called a friend who was dealing with her husband's illness and I supported her in her struggles.

After our conversation, the dishes, laundry, dog-walking, and emailing seemed more like a privilege than a chore. I began to see what's really important: Doing what makes me feel good! Rather than feeling guilty that I wasn't supporting my friend, I took the time to support her. Now we're both more prepared to handle life's challenges. When I feel good, I clearly see my priorities. And when they're done, I have energy left over.

– Marg F.

You'll Never Be Done Again

Take a close look at your to-do list and a quick glance at the piles on the corner of your desk. How much of a backlog do you see? Chances are good that it's a sizeable heap.

According to research reported by David Beardley[1], the average business person faces a backlog of 200 to 300 hours of uncompleted work. That's four to six weeks of slogging; and that number doesn't even begin to consider the projects waiting for us at home or in our communities. It's little wonder you might feel overwhelmed and overloaded on any given day.

> "When I stop caring about the quality of what I'm doing and focus on just getting it done, I know it's time to take a break and come back to the task when I can give it the attention it deserves."
>
> — Teresa Herd

If you find you are disappointed in your performance at the end of every day, stop giving yourself grief because you're not caught up on all of your projects. It isn't going to happen! In fact, getting to the end of your list or reaching the bottom of your pile is an abnormal, extraordinary, and other-worldly experience. Look in the mirror and remind yourself, "You'll never be done again!"

Then check today's to-do list and actions against the backlog to be sure you're acting on what matters most. Credit yourself for the valued tasks you do tackle and complete.

Learn to see a sizeable backlog as a normal fact of life rather than an Everest summit you must conquer every day.

I'm currently on spring break from teaching. Before the break, I organized a pile of work to catch up on during the break. As I left for my break, my principal took my keys away. He told me to go and enjoy my break because I had worked hard these past few weeks. At first I was frustrated and worried about all the files that were due. Now I'm grateful. I feel refreshed and know I'll be a better teacher when I return!

— Renee L.

As a psychologist, I often recommend people slow down in their stressed-out lives, but I realize I don't practice what I preach. Why do we feel as though we need to get everything done in a day? I've decided the only person who's going to take care of me is me, so I'm incorporating brief pauses into my days such as having a cup of coffee and really tasting it, or looking at a picture and really seeing it. I feel a difference already.

— Tania B.

Enough Already

One more phone call.

One more tale.

One more road trip.

One more sale.

It seems that, no matter what happens, we never accomplish, experience, or accumulate enough. Could we be suffering from an expanded sense of what's really necessary?

> "It's not that we are incapable of managing our commitments, but rather that we are unwilling to limit our expectations."
> – Geoffrey Godbey

Sure, goals and dreams and aspirations have their place. They stretch our imaginations and expand our capabilities. But when reaching for loftier goals keeps us from appreciating the present moment, feelings of satisfaction will always be hiding just around the corner.

To increase satisfaction during your day, practice using these short phrases:

"That's enough ... for now."

"That's enough ... for today."

"That's enough ... for the moment."

When you pause and repeat one of these phrases, you let the rare experience of "enough" put the desire for "more" on temporary hold. You needn't worry that you'll lose momentum; reaching and striving will begin again in short order. But just for a moment, pause to enjoy what's already done and won.

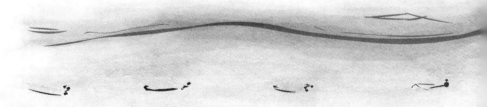

The people we're seeing at this Employee Assistance Program have super-sized workloads and super-sized expectations. Some of them are in trouble. I keep hoping employees will draw a line in the sand and say, 'Enough is enough!' I've started doing that. I'm not working overtime anymore unless a client really needs something!

— Jan N.

My passion is quilting, so I buy all sorts of fabric. But it fills my sewing room to overflowing and gives me more stress than pleasure. My resolve is to give all my fabric to a charity. The clean sweep will make me feel good knowing it will be transformed into living, loving quilts. It will also release all the guilt I feel when I look at unfinished and not-yet-started projects. My go-forward promise is to limit my projects to three: the one I am presently working on, a second in the planning stage, and a third incubating in my head. I feel much lighter already.

— Naomi N.

White Space

Ask people about their most satisfying experiences with time. You might be surprised by their answers. Yes, the pleasure of accomplishment - getting projects done and checking tasks off lists - ranks high. However, you'll find that the experience of unstructured, wide-open chunks of time with no planned activities consistently tops the list.

It's refreshing to have an hour, an afternoon, or a day to putter and ramble - to go where the spirit moves you, not feeling pressured to be anywhere or do anything in particular. Think of this as white space on your calendar - a wide-open chunk of time with no special commitments or duties.

> "Will I remember that the hammock looked good hanging on the front porch or that the garden looked good from the hammock?"
> — LuAnn Brandsen

It's a time when you could invite that new colleague for coffee and conversation or dip into the professional reading that's been piling up in the corner of your office. You might lean over the fence and visit with the neighbors. You could play a round of Monopoly with the kids or snuggle up on the couch with your partner. You could curl up in a hammock with a good book. Or you could simply do nothing at all.

In traditional religious practice, the keeping of the Sabbath assures this recurring openness of time and space. The Sabbath is unique because you don't earn it. It rolls around whether you're ready for it or not.

You can build white space into your work and personal life - for rest, renewal, relationship, or adventure - whether or not it's part of your own tradition. Set a policy of an hour, an afternoon, or an evening each week as open time with no commitments. See what unfolds and develops. Soak up the joy and sense of ease you reap from the experience.

Because my life seems to be so scheduled with deadlines and dates, I find my most satisfying experiences come when I have blocks in which time doesn't matter – like a day I can do what I feel like doing when I want or a vacation with no structure at all. During these times, I enjoy breaking the 'rules' of time. If I want to walk in my garden in my pajamas at 2:00 in the afternoon, I do it, and I relish the fact that I'm breaking a 'rule.' If I want to build a sandcastle at 7:00 in the morning I will, and I dare anyone to tell me it's too early to play on the beach! I'll even work on my stained-glass project until 4:00 in the morning because it's my time.

— Dani V.D.

Late one windless night, with the clear sky brimming with stars, I sat by the barbeque roasting red peppers, a relaxing, carefree release from the norm. Feeling something odd, I noticed there wasn't a sound except the gentle hissing of the barbeque and the popping of the peppers. In our increasingly noisy lives, it was enchanting, peaceful, and somewhat scary to feel and hear the sound of silence.

— Gregg H.

Pull the Plug

Before leaving for his summer vacation, a client left the following message on his voice mail: "Jerome, here. Thanks for calling. As you listen to this, picture me: West Coast, Vancouver Island, Long Beach. Sun in my eyes. Salt spray on my face. Wind in my hair. My wife and my children at my side. As you might guess, I'm on holiday. I have absolutely no intention of calling in for messages. If you need help right away, punch 0 and Maggie will give you a hand. Otherwise, I'll be back in the office on August 22 and will be glad to talk with you then." I chuckled and left a message.

Jerome has learned how to create pauses in his life that let him focus squarely on personal renewal and family relationships. He and his family reap the benefits. His workplace does, too, because he returns to work refreshed and ready to dig in.

> "I have lived too much where I can be reached."
> – Anonymous

"Always on, always connected" may be great for machines. But let's not translate the standing order for accessibility and availability to the humans who own those machines. For a small number of occupations and situations in which survival and safety hang in the balance, the need to stay connected is legitimate. For many more of us, unplugging is a matter of planning and choice.

While down time for machines is considered a bad thing, down time for people is desirable and necessary. Machines have power cords. Humans have belly buttons. We don't plug into a socket in the wall for a recharge while continuing to operate at full strength on power assist.

We need time out and time off. It's how we restore our energy, refocus our attention, and rebuild our enthusiasm. Leave "always on, always connected" to the technology. Resist the pressure to adopt it as your own personal motto and as your expectation for others.

Before taking a month off for a retreat in the country, I asked my friends and family only to send me email that was absolutely necessary. It's been refreshing not to receive those chain letters, jokes, and annoying junk messages. My month of relaxation has been exactly that. I got a much-needed break and realized how much unnecessary stuff I receive every day. I will inform everyone that I no longer want forwarded email messages.

– Linda D.

We don't answer the telephone at meal times – that's our family talk time. We don't answer the telephone during our Friday-night video – that's our family relaxation time. We've been consistent with this for several years now but the first little while was hard. For some reason we felt guilty about not being available for anyone who wanted our time. An answering machine solves that problem. Now we rarely get a phone call during mealtimes.

– Fred H.

MOKALECH

My sisters and I spent Sunday afternoons of my childhood visiting my grandparents. One of my grandmothers was often ill and rested in her bedroom next to the living room. Since five young girls can cause quite a racket, the adults repeatedly cautioned us to be quiet.

Grandma's living room reeked of silence. Heavy furnishings lurked in dark corners. Drapes were drawn tightly against the light of day. The adults spoke in hushed and whispered tones.

> *"We do not remember days, we remember moments."*
> *– Cesare Pavese*

The only exception to the stillness was the mantle clock perched atop the tall antique desk. From one second to the next, it boldly announced the passage of time. Tick ... tick ... tick. Tick ... tick ... tick. In the gloom of that dreary living room, we just knew life was passing us by - one second at a time.

Those visits introduced me to chronos time - the mechanical, consistent, rhythmic passage of time - second by second. Each second is exactly the same as the one before and the one that follows. No more. No less. Tick ... tick ... tick. Tick ... tick ... tick.

> *"Time can stand still, I am convinced of it; something snags and stops, turning and turning, like a leaf on a stream."*
> *– John Banville*

In contrast to the predictable, evenly metered chronos time, the Greek term for time, kairos, suggests some moments are more significant than others. These include the moments of deep engagement, moments of decision, and moments of opportunity. Time may slow, come to a complete halt, or race by in a flash. Kairos moments often mark life's major turning points.

How much of your life do you spend on chronos time, pacing yourself against the relentless ticking of the clock? Spending time.

Saving time. Killing time. In your race to get through the day, do you take advantage of those kairos moments of opportunity?

There's value in the significance of the moment and not just in the rigid marking of the minutes. Think of this as the MOKALECH experience: MOre KAiros, LEss CHronos.

> I'm sitting on the dock at the lake on a comfortably warm and breezy day. I can eventually distract myself from hectic concerns and the to-do list in my mind to enjoy the bugs in the water, the minnows, the fungi on the rock, and the colors and smells of the nearby swamp. The list of beautiful, natural objects becomes endless. Now I see myself and my life in better perspective.
> — Barbara R.

> I've learned that time rarely matters. It's like soft-sided luggage that accommodates as little or as much as I choose to pack. What happens is what happens. There's rarely an occasion when I feel there isn't enough time for what I want to do.
> — Sheryl M.

Vital Vacations

A recent American study[2] of middle-age men at risk for coronary disease found that those who didn't take vacations had a higher risk of death (especially from heart disease) than those who took regular breaks away from work.

It's clear that time off, time out, and time away does a body good! The challenge is to keep from working double time to prepare for the vacation.

For seven years in the earlier years of my career, I wrote a weekly newspaper column. Before every vacation, I'd work like a demon to get ahead on the writing so I could send a bundle of columns to be published in my absence.

> "Sometimes it's important to work for that pot of gold. But other times it's essential to take time off and make sure that your most important decision in the day consists of choosing which color to slide down on the rainbow."
> – Douglas Pagels

Some people take a similar approach to feeding their families. If they're heading off on a vacation or business trip, they burn the midnight oil filling the freezer with casseroles and cookies so their absence is easier for those who depend on them.

Why do we make life unnecessarily tougher by working double time to buy our freedom from routine?

When I recently took my first vacation after starting my weekly ezine, my impulse was to work ahead and fill the gap. In the end, I reminded myself that taking time off is a legitimate and desirable state of affairs for everyone; working double time beforehand defeats the purpose of the vacation.

There's nothing wrong with being missed. There's nothing wrong with others fending for themselves for a while. In fact, in the gap in service, latent talents find room to grow and flourish.

Youngsters may discover they can cook. Colleagues may discover they can handle situations they usually bring to you.

Do your heart a favor and take vacations. Just don't turn the vacation prep into a marathon of its own. ↻

> We're heading out this weekend for two weeks at the lake. It truly restores our souls. My husband needs that place like he needs air and water. It's his center and he spends as much time there as he can. Even if he ends up spending an hour a day on email and phone calls, he's still spending the rest of the time on the lake, getting into trouble with his cousins, and hanging out with the great friends we've made over the years. It truly is his soul.
>
> – Debby C.

Breathing

My yoga instructor asks the same question over and over again, "Are you still breathing?" It's amazing how often the answer is no.

It's good that our bodies have an automatic regulator to keep our lungs going; otherwise we could be turning blue and dropping like flies. Still, there's a huge difference between breathing from the top of the lungs and breathing deeply from the bottom of the diaphragm.

> "Happiness is impossible, and even inconceivable, to a mind without scope and without pause, a mind driven by craving, pleasure, or fear."
> – Santayana

When we get so distracted we forget to take deep breaths, our body suffers. The shoulders roll forward, the chest caves in, the neck tightens, and the jaw sets. Before we know it, we're well on our way to tension headaches or chronic muscle pain.

Since we've become so enamored with multitasking, suppose we combine breathing with a few other tasks such as these:
- Step back from the frenzy.
- Drop your shoulders away from your ears.
- Lean against the door, the wall, the car. Let the world support you for a change.
- Close your eyes for just a moment.
- Take ... one ... deep ... breath.
- Say thanks for a body that still draws breath.
- Smile at nothing in particular.
- Pat yourself on the back for giving yourself a gift of the present.
- Congratulate yourself for taking such good care of your body that you'll be around a long, long time.

Call it a guilt-free breath or a calm-down combo. You're still doing half a dozen things at once - and one of them is relaxing.

I promise myself that I'll look up and stop what I am doing 10 times a day. I'll breathe deeply 10 times and notice details in my surroundings – like the brand new painting I purchased in Newfoundland.
— Catherine B.

What's given me the most benefit for 20 years? Belly breathing. That's it. Nothing more! It's instant, odorless, tasteless, and weightless. It costs little aside from recalling it when I find myself chest breathing. And it prepares me to respond in the right spirit to the material world.
— Rod A.

Artificial Urgency

Do you want to hear a group of bureaucrats gasp in horror? Just suggest that every urgent request for information from a high-ranking government official doesn't constitute an emergency (national security issues and terrorist attacks excluded).

Many things in our lives are serious and important. However, you can gauge a true emergency with one significant test: Is a life in danger? A second test is whether property is in danger.

> "If you treat every situation as a life and death matter, you'll die a lot of times."
> – Dean Smith

Unless you work in health care, law enforcement, or a security-related profession, it's not likely you witness many true emergencies. I know as a writer and speaker, I don't.

In our world, too many issues are unnecessarily presented as urgent. Why? Because we've fallen into the habit of thinking of them that way. We now have access to technology and systems that make instant gratification and overnight service possible. Before we could deliver things so quickly, people and projects rarely had to move fast. Now it seems nothing ever moves fast enough for anyone. Urgencies prevail.

> "The urgent finds you; you have to find the important."
> – Stewart Brand

To experience greater calm and less stress, become more discerning about matters of urgency. Don't react to every situation and request as critical. And don't present them that way to others.

When you next encounter a task stamped Urgent Attention, give it the two-prong emergency test: Danger to life? Danger to property? I'll bet you can count the number of true emergencies you meet in the next few weeks on the fingers of one hand. ↺

Threat to property constitutes an emergency only if you're attached to what you have. I claimed personal bankruptcy and lost everything. Hundreds of people came forward with love and sustenance. I learned that nothing important is attached to property. Everything important is connected to the love of the people and community on my doorstep.

– Laurie P.

My friend, a mother of four young children, had this sign in her kitchen: 'My work is done at 8:00 p.m. Unless it involves blood, have a good evening. See you in the morning.' She really knew how to pause!

– Reva N.

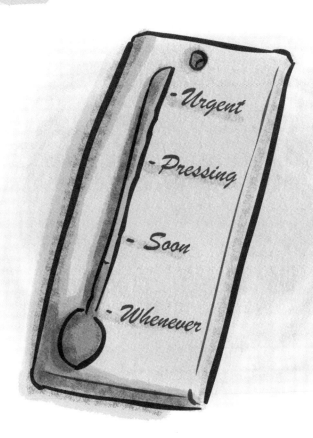

Badges of Honor

From time to time, I have worked with colleagues who sparred for credit by quizzing each other about a variety of issues: How late did your meeting run last night? How many weekends were you on the road? How many vacation days did you carry over? How many miles did you clock on the company car or add to your frequent flyer plan? How many emails were waiting after you returned from vacation? How many minutes did you rack up on your cell phone?

> "If we want our world to be different, our first act needs to be reclaiming time to think. Nothing will change for the better until we do that."
> – Margaret Wheatley

At a seminar, I listened to a panel of work-life balance experts discuss their successes and failures in balancing their own busy lives. They admitted they were challenged to live up to the goals they'd set for themselves. That's true for all of us. Still, the tone of their responses suggested it was okay for their lives to be out of whack because they were doing such important work.

This panel discussion took me back to other conversations in which coworkers measured professional or personal successes in terms of load, distance, sacrifice, and face time. This scale pays little attention to results and none at all to balance.

Eavesdrop on the tone of your own conversations with friends and colleagues when you talk about work-life balance. Is there genuine concern? Do you find and offer support for creative choices, thoughtful boundaries, and sanity-preserving limits? Or do you give lip service to issues of workload, accompanied by a subtle wink-wink-nudge-nudge understanding that important people don't have time for balance and we ought to all just get back to work?

Stars on the epaulettes. Stripes on the shoulders. Pins on the lapels. What badges of honor really matter to you? In our society, what gets honored gets attention. Let's make sure we're tending to the right issues.

We work at jobs that are, at times, highly stressed and quickly changing. We've agreed as a group to look after one another. This is as simple as inviting someone who's feeling snowed under to take a break.

– Lee F.

I gain tremendous satisfaction from my busyness. I love the feeling of contributing and developing personally along the way. When I had down time, I used to fear I was losing my enthusiasm, my spirit. Now in my down time I realize I'm pausing – consciously taking time to think freely about things. I encourage my children to realize the benefit of quiet time when they feel overwhelmed, and I encourage them to pause. I tell them this means 'stop everything' and look, listen, hear, touch, and feel. It's a tool for them and a gift from me.

– Cheryl D.

Cruise Control

As I entered the bathroom, my husband, in mid-shave, leaned close to the mirror and murmured, "Slow down, David!"

He had just raced through his shower to avoid an ice-cold finale. (He was third in line after our teenage daughter and I put a major dint in the hot-water supply.) Partner that race with the high-octane coffee he'd just consumed, and he was buzzing along at top speed - not a safe situation when wielding a sharp razor blade.

> "Pausing is the in-between step. It lies in between our old ways and our new ways."
> — Laura Divine and Joanne Hunt

You might argue he shared responsibility for creating his undesirable situation; he showered last instead of first and chose caffeine over decaf. Still, I admired his ability to notice that he was racing and then to pause and take his foot off the gas.

Pausing is a critical skill in shifting our experience. It's a critical skill in responding differently to stressors in our lives. It's a critical skill in learning new behaviors. You simply can't shift your approach if you're unaware of your current state and unwilling to entertain options.

> "The purpose of stopping is to make the going right."
> — David Kundtz

Watch for situations in which you're racing without a need to do so. Are you racing to catch the phone just because it's ringing? Are you tearing down the hall to a meeting that hasn't yet begun? Are you speeding through dinner when there's no reason to hurry?

Instead, reset your cruise control and enjoy that lower reading on the "frenz-o-meter"! ❧

I'm busy raising a child, running a business, and trying to have a life! I have a wonderful hobby in scrapbooking and am determined to spend more time at it this year. But I find myself rushing to finish each page so I can catch up to the present in my daughter's album. She'll be four years old and I just finished the scrapbook for her first birthday. As I race through each page, I ask, 'What's the rush?' I love to go through the pictures and create wonderful pages filled with special memories. I'm going to stop worrying about how behind I am and enjoy the craft and the camaraderie of the other scrapbookers around me!

— Susan A.

Less Flap... More Focus

Why did the chicken cross the road? Could it be that in her efforts to lay more eggs, the poor bird found herself spinning out of control? Caught up in a frenzy of flapping and fussing, she flew the coop and hit the highway - losing both her why and her way!

It happens. The flying feathers scenario reminds me of a cartoon that features an old-time manager mentoring a newcomer on the need to look busy in the workplace. The old-timer schools the novice in the fine art of rushing and paper-carrying, stressing both are vital to success in the ultramodern, ultrabusy workplace.

> "There are some things I accomplish not by doing but by stopping doing. Creativity, intimacy, growing, and awareness, for example, will not emerge unless I take time out from many of the activities that keep me so busy."
>
> – Anne Wilson Schaef

Given this mindset, it's not surprising that Bruch & Goshal's[3] study of managerial effectiveness concluded that only 10 percent of the managers they studied spent their time in committed, purposeful, and reflective ways. Yikes!

According to these researchers, managerial effectiveness needs two things: (1) focus (targeted action and follow through) partnered with (2) energy (the vigor that comes with strong personal commitment). Distracted managers who pour great gobs

of energy into poorly focused tasks confuse a frenzy of activity - such as briskly carrying papers - with purposeful action.

If you, like the poor misguided chicken or the managers studied by Bruch & Goshal, find yourself running off in all directions with little to show for it, flapping harder may not be your best approach. Slow down, check your position, consult your plan, and rethink your intentions.

Just those simple actions will help you avoid a chicken-with-its-head-cut-off approach to life. All flap, no focus! All fuss, no egg! ෴

> My daughter, Chelsea, worked for a fast-food restaurant. She's a cool, young lady who does what she needs to without fanfare. She's efficient and a quick learner. When it came time for her first evaluation, she was shocked to discover she wasn't going to get a raise. The reason? She didn't look busy enough. She didn't rush about; she walked instead of ran. Fortunately, she had another job, so she quit. With her dignity intact, she went to work for an employer interested in her output rather than her perceived activity level. How many workers did that restaurant train to look busy rather than be efficient and stay cool?
> – Kathy L.

Busyness

So, are you busy? Martin Hayward, a United Kingdom demographer, notes, "Our role models are all busy, busy, busy. The media portrays very important people as never having a spare moment. Our society has this belief that if you're not busy, you're not interesting."

If you subscribe to the "busy is good; busier must be better!" theory, you'll spend a lot of effort racing from one activity to another. After all, the busier you are, the more valuable you think you'll feel.

Now, there's nothing wrong with working hard and getting things done. In fact, achievement can be intensely satisfying, and real progress often springs from superhuman efforts.

However, equal value lives in the quiet moments of life spent on our own or with others. In the stillness, you may reconnect with friends and family, recharge your batteries for the challenges ahead, or simply savor a job well done.

> "We try to possess too much, do too much, and have too many options that are too complex. In the process, there is too little time to think, too little energy left to enjoy."
> – Richard Eyre

To spring yourself from the busyness trap, you'll need to ignore the wisecracks of others: "You're taking a coffee break? Somebody doesn't have enough to do!" Or "What? You're leaving work already? Where can I get a job like that?"

Resist the buzz and barbs. Pause with regularity. Consciously choose a balance of activities that honors your needs for accomplishment as well as relationship and renewal. Give your body a rest and your mind a break. Encourage those around you to do the same.

Always understand that there are moments when nothing means everything.

> Making a list of my tasks for the day helps me remember to schedule relaxation time and activities with my family. Otherwise, I find myself busy with household chores and work. Sometimes I feel I have a million things to do and it causes stress. When I write down specific items on a piece of paper, I often find I have only a few things to do. The list clears my mind and relaxes me. I don't worry about forgetting to do something.
> – Michele H.

Pace Setting

High achievers often set a pace that's tough to match. Highly committed community activists and volunteers may see taking time out for relaxation as a selfish response to a needy world. Workaholics often judge colleagues who take vacations or enjoy rich lives outside the workplace to be slackers who are letting the team down.

I believe each one of us is responsible for making a solid contribution. However, many "communaholics" and workaholics make no distinction between a reasonable contribution and efforts above and beyond the call of duty. They love or believe in what they're doing so much that, for them, work is not a civic or occupational duty. Overtime is the equivalent of hobby time - just more time to play.

> "Balance is not better time management, but better boundary management. Balance means making choices and enjoying those choices."
> – Betsy Jacobson

For these people, work energizes them completely. They find joy and satisfaction in their work. It can, however, be tough on their health and on those around them: fellow volunteers, coworkers, employees, even family members.

When an outstanding level of performance by a workplace or community leader is seen as the minimum standard, others who don't share the same values and interests feel tremendous pressure to measure up. Occasionally, if the leaders can't continue at that high level of performance, they grow tough on themselves and others. A gap between capabilities and expectations develops. Resentments fester.

Are you a high achiever or being pressured by one? If you find yourself caught in this bind, get clear about your values and interests. Talk with others about the differences, then negotiate a reasonable pace and workload for yourself - ones that fit your needs and honor your health and relationships.

As an active workaholic, it's hard to know when to stop — especially when my work is my passion. My passions are community development, my art, and my farming career as well as a wish to recreate my world as I would see it: with gardens, murals, and restored heritage buildings. Rather than not working, I try to remember to lighten up and make my work more playful.

— Janet B.

I realized last night that I felt terrific because, for the first time in a long while, I had no commitments for the evening, no pressing deadlines, nothing to complete for the next day. I could have done dozens of things, but there was nothing I absolutely had to do. I spent the evening with my husband, snug and warm, watching TV and completing a jigsaw puzzle. I have no idea how I can replicate this period of calm between storms, but I'm going to try.

— Jean F.

Raging Bull

I chose a poor day to renew my driver's license. That day, problems with the phone lines made credit and debit card transactions impossible. Customers dug for checks, scrounged for spare change, or dashed down the block to the cash machine.

The cashiers did their best, but progress was slow. A fellow who arrived just moments after I'd entered the queue didn't appreciate the delay. Like a bull in the paddock, he shifted from foot to foot, snorting and pawing the ground. Jingling the change in his pocket and rustling the papers in his hand did nothing to calm his jangling nerves. Neither the repeated checks of his wristwatch nor the disgusted glares he zinged at the cashiers brought him relief.

> "The greatest power is often simple patience."
> – E. Joseph Cossman

A few minutes after his arrival, a newcomer fell in line behind the restless rustler. In the loudest possible voice, the raging bull cautioned her that he hoped she'd brought a book and planned to spend the day because he'd been waiting in line all morning!

In less than five minutes, it was my turn at the counter. I leaned in close to the cashier and told her I hoped she had 911 on her speed dial; I thought our friend, the raging bull, was about to pop an artery. She chuckled and rolled her eyes, clearly relieved to connect with an understanding customer who showed a sense of humor.

> "Blessed are the flexible for they shall not be bent out of shape."
> – Michael McGriffy

Life is full of delays and detours. We shouldn't be surprised when life doesn't unfold as expected. Forget snorting and pawing the ground. Look for the humor around you. Empathize with others caught in the bind. You can always find a response that will be far more helpful than a frustrated, raging bull reaction.

Our expectations fuel the spiral we're all in. Change will come about when each of us makes the conscious decision to relax our expectations of everyone around us. We must realize that every time we expect instant service, response, food, and entertainment, we're validating all of the instant demands made on us.

The golden rule defines what will save us from ourselves: Do unto others as you would have them do unto you. What would happen if irate customers in line at the bank, food outlet, or post office would think about how they'd feel if they were the ones serving that line of impatient, rude, and irate customers. Maybe they'd cut some slack for the poor sots who are trying their best to make everyone happy.

– Debby C.

Stop-Sign Buddies

Red lights and stop signs signal our preoccupation with getting somewhere fast - those lights and signs often seem to work against us and in favor of oncoming traffic.

When you're on the highway, you're sure to find yourself stuck behind a slow-moving vehicle. Slow, of course, is a relative concept. When you're in a rush, slow may mean that the vehicle ahead is "just" driving the speed limit. With more multilane highways and passing lanes, slow-moving traffic is less of a problem than it was during the days of single-lane highways. In those days you could find yourself stuck behind an Airstream trailer convoy for hours.

Still, for most of us, patience isn't a strong point in our high-speed, nonstop world. Finding ourselves stalled at a red light for a few seconds or stuck behind a vehicle for a few minutes seems like hours.

> "The idea is not to slow life down, but to calm it down."
> – Jim Tunney

It doesn't have to be that way. In his essay "Driving Meditation,"[4] Thich Nhat Hanh describes travel delays such as red lights and stop signs as gifts. He suggests that these delays serve to keep us from rushing ahead of ourselves. They return us to the present moment. In a similar vein, some of the traffic lights in Delhi, India, have the word Relax written across the red light, rather than the old British stoplights that read Stop.

Yes, it's a mind shift to embrace delays and slowdowns in a positive light. Give it a try the next time you hit the road. Who knows what you might discover when you slow down enough to appreciate your journey as much as you appreciate reaching your destination?

I live in an area where trains frequently cross — and they seem to always cross when I'm in a hurry. My level of frustration increases with each passing boxcar on the tracks. One day I had a novel in the van. I picked it up while waiting for the train. The wait didn't seem like an eternity. Instead, the five minutes flew by and I wished I had more time to read my book. Now I keep something interesting in the vehicle to read so my waiting time is more enjoyable.

— Catherine G.

The other day I started a practice of sending love to every person I see when I'm driving. As I put the notion into motion with a person who was crossing the street in front of me, I found my heart softening and my breathing changing. My body grew more relaxed and my head felt differently. I'm aiming to make this practice a constant, reflexive habit. I believe it will make a difference in my little world and in the larger world as well: gentleness and compassion rather than hurry and self-centeredness.

— Corinne A.

Courage

Do you feel pressure to meet the expectations of others? I do.

I declined a speaking opportunity that conflicted with a commitment I'd already made to accompany my daughter's class on a field trip. The potential client told me I was out of my mind to turn down business.

My daughter opted out of an expensive excursion for her choir because it didn't fit with our family plans and financial goals. We felt pressured to reconsider our decision throughout the entire choral season.

> "Courage is not the absence of fear but rather the judgment that something else is more important than fear."
> – Ambrose Redmoon

An experienced teacher struggled to find the courage to ask permission to skip the last afternoon of a teacher's convention. She desperately wanted to catch a flight that would allow her to hold her new granddaughter in her arms for the first time. Yet she shook in her boots at the thought of making this request to her director of education.

Fighting the relentless pressures of a culture filled with expectations for our lives is like swimming upstream. It takes conviction and confidence to move beyond external pressures - to know and speak our minds. Part of life's challenge is finding the courage to honor our own needs and preferences.

It takes space and time for your own voice and thoughts about who you are, who you could be, and what you need to rise to the top of your awareness.

Be courageous. Be present to the needs of the moment. Take personal responsibility to determine what fits for you, your organization, and your family. Enjoy your choices. Pause to learn from each experience so you can keep creating your most desirable future.

I've worked as a commissioned salesperson for 20 years and the rule is: 'the client rules.' About six years ago, a trainer forced me to take a day off from selling each week and stick to it. I struggled with the command. But it was the best thing I ever did! I learned how to say, 'I'd love to discuss this with you and can we do it on such-and-such day?' I haven't lost any business and I've gained one day a week that I know is mine. It's rejuvenating, invigorating, and life saving.

— Jane M.

Last weekend, I took an extra day off and created a long weekend during a hectic time at work. My three-month-old niece was home with my sister from Vancouver. The time I spent with my family, especially the newest addition, helped me focus on what was important. When I got back to the office, I didn't seem so busy after all. It was just stuff to do!

— Margot W.

Lingering

Part of my Yuletide tradition is to play Garrison Keillor's album "Now It Is Christmas Again"[5] while I mix up a batch of cinnamon buns on Christmas Eve.

The final verse of my favorite song on the album is:

> We said goodbye in the hallway
> We said goodbye on the stair
> We said goodbye on the sidewalk in the cold December air
> We leaned against the cars and we said goodbye out there
> At the Sons of Knute Christmas dance and dinner.

Multistage farewells with friends, family, and neighbors are familiar recollections from my childhood. It didn't matter whether the visit had been short (just dropping in for coffee) or whether it had lasted all day and evening (sharing meals, card games, and conversation). The extended departures weren't a matter of social awkwardness. People simply enjoyed each other's company and felt reluctant to part ways.

> "The best things said come last. People will talk for hours saying nothing much and then linger at the door with words that come with a rush from the heart."
> – Alan Alda

In short, they lingered. We don't linger much anymore these days. It's a shame. Lingering is a savory, sensory experience. A lingering scent on the air. A lingering kiss on the lips. A lingering arm around the shoulder. A lingering smile or handshake.

Why not resurrect the practice of lingering? Extend meaningful experiences for a shade longer: the hellos, the goodbyes, and all the special exchanges in between. Dwell in the moment. Soak up the sights, the tastes, the touches, the sounds.

Linger now and the memories will linger later.

As a landscape architect and urban designer for 30 years, I've been doing my best to design and build urban spaces that encourage people to linger and pause – to sit, chat, wait, browse, read, munch, smell flowers, enjoy a view, people-watch, touch various materials, hear or glimpse urban wildlife, share and feel the cool shade of a magnificent tree, and generally feel more comfortable in our usually indifferent and carelessly built environments. There's much challenge ahead in a dominant culture whose laws frequently prohibit loitering in public spaces.

– Bela B.

I recommend watching birds now and then, just for a minute. I found myself doing this the other morning (thanking them for every crabapple they ate off my tree). It was wonderfully mesmerizing and centering. Sad to say, it takes awareness to think to slow down even that long, but it's worth it!

– Corinne A.

Magnanimity

As I listen to reports of life's daily events, I witness indignation, wailing, and gnashing of teeth over supposed slights and imagined dastardly deeds. Yes, I even catch myself engaging in these flights of fancy from time to time.

Sometimes an illness is just an illness - not something caused by careless hygiene, dubious nutrition, or medical malpractice. Sometimes lost keys and bank cards are misplaced - not the work of a stealthy thief with sticky fingers. Sometimes an offhand remark is just plain thoughtless - not part of a diabolical plot to undermine our authority or self-esteem. Talk about blowing things out of proportion!

> "Be kind. Everyone you meet is fighting a hard battle."
> – John Watson

At the same time, much of the stress that leads someone to behave badly remains invisible to others. We aren't always privy to each others' burdens: an angry client, an ailing parent, a truant teen, a leaky roof, a dwindling bank account, a frightening medical report, an estranged friendship.

> "If you want others to be happy, practice compassion. If you want to be happy, practice compassion."
> – Dalai Lama

Let's be more magnanimous with ourselves and each other. It's a great word for stressful times: magnanimous refers to a loftiness of spirit that helps one bear trouble calmly. It means "to scorn meanness and revenge."

Put more simply, magnanimity (another mouthful) is a generosity of mind. It means cutting someone slack, extending the benefit of the doubt.

Maybe the driver who cut you off is on the way to a medical emergency. Maybe the person who hasn't returned your phone call didn't receive your message. Maybe the sales clerk who overcharged you for an item is adjusting to a new pair of glasses.

These possibilities are worth considering when you're about to hold someone's feet to the fire - including your own. More magnanimity, please! ↻

> We had a surprise blizzard today – severe and short-lived – yet it caused another death on the highway. I was totally stressed out. I had to perform home-care chores for my elderly mother because the regular home-care provider couldn't travel. I wanted to order a pizza and discovered the restaurant was opening an hour later. I tried to be cordial to the pleasant waitress, even though I was upset. When I returned home, I read your message about being more magnanimous. I immediately called June, the waitress, to tell her the pizza was super and we enjoyed it. Thanks to observing the 'M' word, I'm still smiling brightly. I'm sure June is as well.
>
> – Gregg H.

Margins

Imagine this page with text spilling off the edges. Imagine a schedule crammed solid with meetings from morning to night. Imagine your clothes fitting so tightly you don't have room to breathe. Imagine a car without bumpers. The result? No place to rest your eyes, no ease, no grace, no protection from the bumps and bruises of life.

Life without buffers. Dr. Richard Swenson[6] suggests that in our preoccupation with speed and progress, we sacrifice our margins. Margin is that difference between your load and your limits, such as physical and emotional energy, finances, and time. Think of it as the reserve space, or leeway, in your life.

> "Those who are caught up in the busy life have neither the time nor the quiet to come to understand themselves and their goals. Since the opportunity for inward attention hardly ever comes, people have not heard from themselves for a long, long time. Those who are always 'on the run' never meet anyone any more, not even themselves."
> – Robert Banks

Living a just-in-time existence at the edge of your resources can be exciting, but it comes at a price. It leaves no cushion for tough times, surprises, unexpected problems, or opportunities. And, as any high-speed adventurer knows, if you crash without padding, you'll know pain on a first-name basis.

Do you know and honor your own limits? When you handle resources of time, money, or energy, at what point do you shift

from swimming with strength, confidence, and direction to desperately treading water - and then drowning? Even tiny margins (a few extra minutes, a few extra dollars, or a few extra winks of sleep) can make a big difference in how fast and how often you hit bottom.

Build in margins in small, doable ways. Leave a few minutes early for your next appointment. Stop working on a project before you reach the point of complete exhaustion. Make your next purchase well within your means rather than pushing to the outside limit of your bank account. ↷

> A 'pause' sticker on my computer reminds me to slow down and take a breath. I take a few minutes in the morning to reflect on how I want to spend my day. I take a few more minutes at the end of the day to jot down notes for the next day. It saves time in the long run but also gives me a sense of control. I'm more aware now of what I can control (me and my attitude) and what I can't control (pretty much everything else in my life). I'm less defensive when others claim they're too busy to take breaks during the day. They say this with a note of superiority as though their time is too valuable or their work is too important. My brain works better if it gets to take a break.
>
> – Andrea A.

Presence

Bill is my favorite grocery clerk. I'll wait in Bill's checkout line even though it may be a cart or two longer than the next lane. Why? Because Bill is the real deal. He's an original spirit who brings life and laughter to a boring, mundane experience.

> "Your presence and perspective are as important as your skills."
> – Geoffrey Bellman

Some cashiers offer a curt hello with no eye contact. They're preoccupied with checking out the rest of the store while mindlessly checking out your groceries. Not Bill. He pauses to give you his full attention as he greets you with a smile. He's lively, affable, and conversant about the events of the day. He'll even hazard a guess at your dinner plans based on the ingredients flying across the scanner.

Bill's no speedier than any other clerk. And he isn't more accurate than any other clerk. But one thing is patently clear: Bill shows up every day ready to be nowhere else. Do you?

> "The tragedy of life is not so much what men suffer, but rather what they miss."
> –Thomas Carlyle

You have an opportunity to shine in your everyday environment and make the most of every encounter. But you'll succeed only if you are present to what's going on right under your nose. Do you really see that client? Do you hear that colleague? Do you acknowledge that stranger?

Your presence is a gift you bring to others, a gift that returns big dividends. Your whole, true self is a key part of your success. Don't leave home without it. And don't send it off on errands while you're busy doing something else!

When traveling, I've discovered that when I reached my destination, I couldn't remember going through certain towns. I was thinking about what I had to do when I reached my destination. If I had taken the time to enjoy the drive, I would've been more relaxed at the end of it.

— Pat S.

My most satisfying experiences are when I'm conversing with a friend and time seems to stand still. I get an incredible feeling of connection from active listening and staying in the moment. We leave the experience feeling closer to each other, satisfied, and at peace that a deeper understanding has occurred.

— Gina W.

I was on my way to a meeting. My son needed some time with me and I took 10 minutes to be fully present with him. It was a moment of knowing. When I only have right now, the immediate moment, I have all the time in the world. This insight hit me like a ton of bricks.

— Ruth K.

Surrendering

Do you think of yourself as a take-charge person? Master of your fate? Captain of your destiny? If you're like me, sometimes your plans and dear old destiny aren't on the same wavelength. In those instances, it's not unusual to keep pushing, hoping destiny will yield. But, this seldom works! Destiny is a slippery, ornery cuss!

The opposite choice, backing off, may feel like weakness. But choosing to surrender can be a good thing. If you've ever fallen helplessly, happily in love, you know what I mean.

> "In an easy and relaxed manner, in a healthy and positive way, in its own perfect time."
> – Marc Allen

Surrendering works in other arenas, too. My most satisfying convention experience involved simply letting go. Instead of structuring every moment, I set one key objective, chose two must-see sessions, and went with the flow. Every person I met and every session I attended offered insights directly related to my key business problem. I didn't seek them out. They just showed up. In this case, releasing control paid big dividends.

Every day brings opportunities to push and press or to surrender and let things unfold in their own sweet time. Experiment and observe. See what you can learn about shifting between action and inaction to meet your challenges of the moment.

I went away for a week of relaxation, writing, and a little family time. I ended up with a week that was all family time, with very little relaxation, and no writing. Half way through the week, I decided to go with the flow. I love my son, daughter-in-law, and two little grandsons. I spent time playing and building memories that will last the rest of my life. Who knows where the next minutes take us? I continually remind myself to be in the moment.

— Laurie P.

Our four children went camping with Grandma and Grandpa, leaving my wife and me alone for the day. Our intention was to accomplish a lot that day, but the day didn't unfold as planned. As we drove by our neighbors' house, we saw them sitting in lawn chairs in front of their garage in the shade. We stopped to say a quick hello and visited with them for two hours. Our visit changed our plans to get a lot done, but it was one of the best visits we've had with these friends. For the rest of the day, rather than try to make up for lost time, my wife and I decided we would spend time together and not feel guilty about not 'doing.' It was wonderful!

— Jerome N.

"Unitasking"

A business man races through the Denver airport towing his suitcase with one hand, briefcase and coat balanced precariously on top. His "free" hand, held near one ear, grips his boarding card and cell phone. Deep in conversation and oblivious to his surroundings, he steps on an escalator that, instead of taking him down one floor, dumps him back where he started. Without missing a beat, he steps back on the same escalator with, of course, the same result.

> "Maintaining a complicated life is a great way to avoid changing it."
> – Elaine St. James

A mind-racing, self-professed Efficiency Queen often thinks about something in the future while doing something else in the present. In the heat of an intimate moment with her husband, she blurts out this phrase: "Man, those bagels are going to taste good in the morning!"

A frenzied mother teaches her teenage daughter to take her dinner plate to the counter and eat standing up so the girl can empty the dishwasher and finish dinner at the same time.

Three real people. Three real events. All three actions share one belief: it's a waste of time to do only one thing at once. Multitasking rules!

Sometimes multitasking makes sense. Most times it doesn't. In fact, doing many things at the same time can be hazardous to your safety, your relationships, and your sanity.

The key is to become conscious about your actions and the impact of your behavior. Choose the moments when you split your concentration. Recognize the value in focusing on just one thing or one person. "Unitasking" is sometimes the wisest choice of all.

It works to take a few extra seconds to connect with the person you're with. I tried it this morning with a frustrated customer. We ended up having a good laugh. He shook my hand when he left and said, 'I finally found someone who cares about my situation.'
— Kathy D.

My favorite 'pause' moments occur when I tuck my son into bed at night and he reads me a bedtime story. He's in third grade and loves to read. We've invested in a series of simple books he can read out loud. This helps his skills, encourages his love of reading, and helps me remember how wonderful I used to feel as a child hearing a bedtime story. Best of all, it's a quiet moment we share together getting lost in another land that doesn't involve TV, video games, school, work, or outside pressures.
— Jennifer B.

Wabi Sabi

According to a Priority Management survey[7] of 3,000 North Americans, Europeans, and folks from "Down Under," only 5 percent report that they feel a sense of personal accomplishment at the end of each day.

Even though 80 percent of these respondents work more than 40 hours a week, 95 percent of the executives, administrators, and employees surveyed head out the door at day's end feeling disappointed in themselves.

Are you one of those 95 percent?

> "Instead of looking at what we don't have and aren't, we need to look at ourselves and each other, enjoy what we have, and celebrate who we are."
> — Pamela McKenna

If this sense of "dis-ease" affects you, take a close look at your expectations. It's no longer reasonable to expect to be caught up at the end of any given day or have completed every task to perfection. The best we can hope for is to make reasonable progress on the projects that have the highest level of priority.

The Japanese phrase wabi sabi describes the ability to find joy and beauty in things incomplete, imperfect, and impermanent. This concept is worth cultivating.

Think of it this way: No, the project isn't done but you handled tasks that moved it forward. No, you didn't reach every person on your phone list but you left messages for most of them. No, you aren't caught up on the laundry but everyone in your family has something clean to wear tomorrow.

You and I can harvest satisfaction on even the most wabi sabi of days.

My coach discovered two amazing things about me. First, I never stop to celebrate the good things as they happen. And second, my definitions of good and fun are far too narrow. I don't have to wait to celebrate the completion of a project; I can celebrate making a single phone call that will contribute to the completion of the project.

My life has turned around in two weeks. I now stop every four or five hours and tick off my successes of the past few hours. This grounds me in the present time rather than always looking to the future and pushing forward. I feel better about picking up the load and moving forward again.

— Wayne G.

Focus Time

For a decade, two close friends and I have observed what we call balance days. We book one day at the turn of each season (four days a year) to spend together so we can focus on renewal and work-life balance issues.

> "We do not need volume, we need focus."
> – Jerry Paulson

We've picnicked, played, and taken long walks. We've treated ourselves to massages and other spa treats. We've cried on each other's shoulders and picked each other up. On each winter solstice, we book a shared day of silence at a local retreat center. Always, we share our insights and our challenges on the journey to greater work-life balance. This practice and our commitment to each other strengthen our resolve and our results.

In my business, I've made it a practice to pause regularly - to learn from the past and invest in the future. I celebrate my successes. I look clearly at how and where I continue to trip myself up. I harvest the lessons in workload management from the previous months. I think about the next few months and anticipate what I need to do differently.

> "Every once in a while, you have to give yourself a chance to stop, to empty out. Taking time off allows you space to let the big ideas in."
> – Derek Bullen

Each time I make this investment in focus time, I reap the rewards. When I don't build it in, I scramble - doomed to repeat the same mistakes *ad nauseum*.

What kind of focus time can you build into your life? How can you solidify your progress and shift to a more satisfying balance of work and renewal? ❧

During the work day, I am constantly interrupted with faculty, students, and staff. If I can secure one uninterrupted hour, I can clear away a load of tasks in a hurry. I accomplish more by starting with the really tough and dreaded tasks, leaving the easy stuff. Sometimes, I don't even get to the easy stuff and it just disappears.

– Alison R.

My attitude at the beginning of the day is important to me. I need time to read, reflect, and choose one or two key actions for that day. It's easier for me to keep my day in perspective when I've reflected on the day's events before I fall asleep. I apply the same principle to my year. In the middle of a difficult week, I reflect on the entire year and it puts my week into perspective. I recognize the many positive opportunities for growth and enjoyment that have occurred and the negativity diminishes.

– Cathy V.

Lock-On Listening

A colleague and mentor of mine is an exceptional communicator. Even though we only briefly connect in person once a year at an annual conference, our relationship grows stronger with every exchange.

We typically find a quiet corner out of the line of traffic. We sit knee to knee, speak eye to eye, with our backs to the commotion in the hallways. Though our conversations are short, the exchange is powerful. Time is irrelevant.

> "Speed, in and of itself, has never improved the dialogue between humans – quite the contrary could be argued, given that haste so often impedes accuracy, reflection, and perspective."
> – John R. MacArthur

Conversations on the run are a normal part of our busy lives, but they may not always be as effective as the exchange I just described. Neuroscientists find that when people feel rushed, they're more likely to experience a standing conversation as less genuine than a seated exchange. Perhaps with both parties on their feet and poised for action, it feels as though either partner could bolt at any second.

To increase the power of your everyday communication with others, slow down and let the other person know you really care about making the connection.

If time is short, note how long you can spend. State this in a positive way, for example, "I have five minutes; let's make the most of it."

Find a perch that puts you both at the same eye level for the duration of the exchange. Take a breath. Pause before you jump in with a hasty comment or quick response. Look directly at your partner. Ignore the commotion around you and, above all, stop checking your watch.

Lock on. Listen intently. Let your instincts tell you when five minutes are up. You'll be surprised how time stretches and relationships grow when you pay attention to the person - not the clock. ↻

> I went to lunch with a friend I haven't seen in a while. We're both struggling with our own issues. She's a stepparent to teenage children and facing serious health problems. Her husband's career is in jeopardy and she's deciding whether to apply for her dream job. I'm juggling a career that involves a great deal of travel, raising two young girls, and supporting a husband whose self-employment is like riding a roller coaster – all while facing the symptoms of early menopause. Even with focusing on all this, we had a wonderful lunch. We poured out our hearts and souls, and both left feeling better than we had when we arrived. We're so lucky to be able to talk, listen, share stories, and not 'solve' each other's problems. I value my friend and I'm glad to have her in my life.
> – Lori P.

Pep Breaks

Aside from lunch, the most common pause in the typical work day is the sit-down coffee break. These mid-morning and mid-afternoon breaks were originally negotiated by labor unions on behalf of steel workers and miners who engaged in backbreaking physical labor. Taking a sit-down break restored muscle strength and renewed the physical energy they needed to keep working.

These days, most of us are far removed from swinging sledgehammers and pickaxes. Much of the physically challenging work has been automated. Most work in today's Information Age is sedentary. People who sit most of the day at work tend to strain two parts of the anatomy: their bottoms and their brains. These need attention.

> "Each of us needs to withdraw from the cares which will not withdraw from us. We need hours of aimless wandering or spates of time sitting on park benches, observing the mysterious world of ants and the canopy of treetops."
> – Maya Angelou

To make your "coffee" breaks more energizing, think "contrast". If you sit all day, move. If you're stuck indoors, get outside. If you're surrounded by people, technology, and general commotion, seek time alone. If you're dealing with serious issues, find a way to laugh and let off steam.

Experiment with shorter, more frequent pep breaks and you'll multiply their effectiveness. When you choose contrasting breaks at more frequent intervals, both bottom and brain will return to work rejuvenated - and you'll have more zip left at the end of your work day. ☙

I work in a school that has kindergarten to grade 12. When I have time, I spend some of my lunch hour on the playground – playing, sliding, and swinging. When I get busy, I work through lunch. I don't have time to play and I miss it. Lately, I've gotten back into playing, especially on the days I'm busy and stressed. Within my first minute outside, stress drains out my toes and the tension leaves. I come back relaxed, recharged, and ready to take on the rest of the day.

– Carla P.G.

If I set my watch alarm and get up to stretch, taking a five-minute walk away from my computer, it helps my blood pressure and promotes calmness. I often do five-minute meditations. On occasion, I open an inspirational message and play music on my computer.

– Sharon H.

My most successful strategy for building in pauses is to leave my work space at lunch time. I usually exercise with a couple of buddies. We spend time joking about our aging bodies and groan about doing the exercise. This is refreshing for me. I come back to my desk ready to work.

– Sue M.

Targets

Have you ever promised those who are important in your life (including yourself) that you'll have time for them soon? Soon is a nebulous time that never seems to roll around.

Setting targets can shift the balance. Try these approaches: Set one date a week with your partner, plan a special monthly event with each of your youngsters, hold Monday nights for a yoga class (no exceptions), or reserve Friday evenings as veg-out time.

Take the same approach in the professional arena. Don't let promises to learn that new software program fall by the wayside. Book an appointment with yourself for the first half hour every Thursday and work your way through the tutorial 30 minutes at a time for the next six weeks.

> "When I don't take the time to figure out what I want, I am sentenced to doing what others want."
> – Geoffrey Bellman

Are you losing touch with colleagues or employees? Make lunch on Friday your plug-in point. Invite a different colleague to join you each week. Use the time to strengthen each of those relationships.

Choose what works for you. Create your own targets for connection, development, and renewal. Enter your target activities in your calendar and honor them as you would any high-priority commitment. ↻

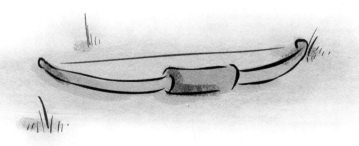

As the single mom of a spirited seven-year-old boy I sometimes feel overwhelmed, stressed, tired, and frustrated. When I hit a low, I declare a pajama day with my son. Other than staying in our pajamas all day, there are no rules – no phone calls, no work, no computer, no cooking, nothing that consists of using our brains! We do frivolous things – eating all the ice cream we have and watching crazy cartoons and movies, playing cards and checkers, listening to music, dancing ourselves silly, and then eating more ice cream. It doesn't cost anything. And we don't have to put our pajamas back on at the end of the day.

– Lynda C.

I enjoy painting and drawing, but my hobby faltered when I graduated college. I missed the calm and relaxation that doing art provides and could feel my creativity waning. This fall, I enrolled in a Thursday-night art class. I also attend an artist's workshop every Saturday morning for three hours. I'm proud that I take the time for me. When I'm in my classes, all the worries and pressures of life float away!

– Kristal W.M.

Rituals

Rituals are powerful. Hello/goodbye, good morning/good night kisses are an everyday occurrence in my marriage. Leave takings with our daughters - by phone or in person - are punctuated from both sides with the phrase, "Love ya." Our dinner grace includes a "today I am thankful for ..." comment from each person around the table.

As with brushing your teeth in the morning, these actions and phrases have become second nature. That doesn't make them meaningless. Each exchange expresses deeply held values of love and appreciation.

> "Rituals provide a level of comfort, continuity, and security that frees us to improvise and to take risks."
> – Jim Loehr and Tony Schwartz

Rituals bring our values to life. If you value your health, turning a lunchtime walk into an automatic ritual breathes life into that value. If you value family, the ritual of a weekly phone call with a parent or sibling keeps the connection alive. If you value the beauty of nature, the ritual of placing freshly cut flowers on your desk or your table keeps nature in the center of your everyday life. You get the picture.

What kind of rituals are already working for you? What other rituals could you create to shift more of your deeply held values from intention to action?

Tie those practices to a specific time or place. Build them into your daily or weekly routines. Watch the impact!

When I turn on my computer each day at the office, I stop and think, 'What is the priority of the day?' I tell myself I'm only one person and can do only so much. I then go about my day. If I start to sink, I stop, pause, and remind myself what I said first thing in the morning. That usually brings me back into perspective.

— Donna C.

My big moment came when I decided to go back to my habit of reading books before bedtime. I finish my evening tasks at least half an hour before bedtime. This creates a definite end to the day and a sense of control. Reading prepares me for a good night's sleep because it requires me to disconnect from the day. My breathing slows down. My enjoyment of the moment goes up. I do this by myself, for myself. And I can't wait for the following night so I can find out what happens next.

— Jane M.

Sanity Policies

In the early years of my business, I worked many weekends and often delivered an all-day seminar followed by an evening presentation. As burnout loomed, I chose a policy of working just one weekend a month, speaking and training no more than three days a week, and presenting in only two out of three time slots on a given day (morning, afternoon, or evening).

> "If there are one hundred good things to do and you can only do ten of them, you will have to say no ninety times."
> – Richard Swenson

My productivity and energy soared. Amazingly, so did my profits. Clearly, taking care of myself was also good for my business.

Community service is another area where overload shifts the experience from blessing to burden. How many community groups can you serve at a time and still feel enthused as you head out the door to another evening meeting?

If you're frustrated en route, you'll feel less than enthusiastic at the meeting itself. Rest assured, if you don't want to be there and can't wait to get away, you aren't the ray of sunshine that will brighten the day for others.

> "A 'no' uttered from the deepest conviction is better than a 'yes' merely uttered to please, or what is worse, to avoid trouble."
> – Mahatma Gandhi

Know yourself. Draw your lines in the sand. Stand by your decisions. Set your own sanity policies for paid and volunteer work. Stake your claim. Make time for renewal and relaxation. All of these will help you stay productive and enthused so you can make a positive contribution over the long term.

I decided to give up volunteering. It sounds terrible but I'm 34 years old, work part-time, and have two sons who are seven and ten. My children are busy with music and sports and my husband works long hours and coaches in our sons' hockey organizations. This leaves me to run all aspects of our home life. I felt pressure to volunteer - to do my part. But I didn't enjoy it. As a result, I didn't put forward a proper effort or attitude. I decided that my job is raising my two sons to be happy, well-rounded young men. They'll remember sharing time with their mother who was there when they needed her, not at some meeting. There will be lots of time to volunteer when my sons are grown. I feel positive that I've set a good boundary!

— Tiffany J.S.

"Simplicizing"

I have an irksome habit (and I have it in spades) - stuffing too much in! One more email. One more stop on the way. One more point in the presentation.

The motivation is good: squeeze maximum value out of each moment. However, the result is bad: time pressure and frustration, for me and for others.

Being more judicious about biting off more than we can comfortably chew is good for our health. Becoming more thoughtful and reasonable in all areas of life also brings positive changes to our mental health and our relationships.

> "More, more, more, more. My hell, what are we all, morticians?"
> – Richard Eyre

A speaker colleague edits his presentations by keeping his audience and this question in mind: "What could they live without?" This question can be applied far and wide. Whether it's our work, errands, or communications, we can ask ourselves, "What could we (or they) live without?"

With the enormous proliferation of email, think twice before sending a message into circulation. Will it add value? Will anyone read it? Will the other person's world be better with this communication? Sometimes less is more.

How relaxed would we feel if we squeezed fewer tasks into every moment? Or if we became more creative about handling the overload?

A college dean returned from an extended vacation and found 3,000 email messages in her inbox. She made an initial effort to sift and sort, then sent them all to trash. She took her staff members out for coffee to catch up in person. In the end, about 20 messages were significant and their senders came looking for a response. That is creative "simplicizing" at its best!

As my husband and I paused in the hot tub one evening under sparkling stars, our conversation ran to the practice of stream of consciousness writing recommended in Julia Cameron's *The Artist's Way*[8]. My husband has implemented the practice and mentioned that sometimes he'd write a list of things to do. When he reviewed the list later, he realized most of the things didn't really need to be done. We have a suggestion for an alternate use of lists. Make a list. Reflect on whether the completed items will make a difference. Act only on those for which the answer is yes.

– Geri B.

I had a bad habit of taking calls as I was leaving the office at the end of the day. Often, the call required immediate follow up on an issue and delayed my departure. Now I don't take calls as I make my way out of the office. I have more control over my departure time.

– Sandra C.

Plimsoll Line

In the mid-19th century, greedy British ship owners overloaded their cargo holds and gleefully pocketed the insurance profits when the ships foundered and sank. Many sailors lost their lives on these "coffin" ships.

> "We can easily manage if we will only take, each day, the burden appointed to it. But the load will be too heavy for us if we carry yesterday's burden over again today, and then add the burden of the morrow before we are required to bear it."
> – John Newton

Samuel Plimsoll waged a battle against this practice. As a result, the Merchant Shipping Act of 1876 decreed that all cargo vessels must display the Plimsoll line - a line painted on the side of the ship indicating the safe, legal loading limit. Why is this line necessary? Because ships float at different levels depending on the warmth and consistency of the water. A ship loaded to capacity in a North Atlantic salt-water port is in danger of riding too low and possibly sinking at a fresh-water port in the tropics.

What does this have to do with you? Modern-day individuals and organizations have their limits, too. Wouldn't it be cool if we each carried a Plimsoll line? You'd know exactly when you were reaching your stability limit, and you could see the current state of those around you.

Of course, we don't come equipped with Plimsoll lines. But

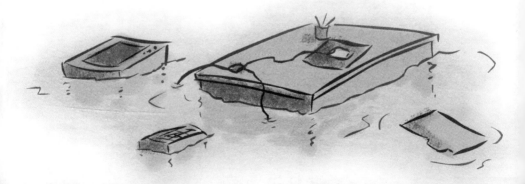

these modern indicators might offer clues to individual load and capacity:

- Physical strength and wellbeing - Are your body and mind in top condition or suffering from illness and fatigue?
- Buoyancy - Are emotional and practical supports in place or have you lost an important caregiver or mentor?
- Security - Are expectations constantly shifting and sliding or are the key elements of your load stable?
- Weights and measures - Do you know how long tasks will take? How critical are the outcomes? Will you see a definite end to the leg of a journey?
- Renewal - Is your load incessant and heavy or can you spend time in "dry dock" for repairs, rest, and refurbishment?

Pay close attention to how low you and your colleagues are riding in the water on any given day.

> We reshuffled job responsibilities last November and I'm assessing the Plimsoll line for each of my employees. I'm looking at their eyes when we discuss work and workloads; at their postures - are their shoulders round and stooped or are they eager and energetic; and at how long they stay - people are asking to work overtime, which isn't a good sign. We're still on top of everything, but at what price? I want to bring relief to my employees before the workload starts to affect their performance.
>
> – Wayne G.

Empty or Full?

How much gas is in your tank? On a scale of one to ten, how energized do you feel at this moment? One: your tank is dry. Ten: it's topped off and brimming over.

Noticing is an essential first step in managing this important resource: personal energy. Responding is the second step. As my dad used to caution, "Always drive on the top half of the tank. That way you've got reserves if you get into trouble."

If your energy reserve is low, what would it take to top off your tank - or at least raise the level an inch or two? Have you focused too long on one task and need a change? Have you been sitting too long and need to stretch your legs? Are you feeling dried out and spent, in need of something to drink or eat? Have you abandoned your enthusiasm because you've lost track of the reason you're working on this project? Are you feeling numb and disconnected from yourself or others?

> "Inside myself is a place where I live all alone, and that's where I renew my springs that never dry up."
> – Pearl Buck

Make it a practice to repeatedly check your fuel gauge through the day. Then choose small actions to "fillerup" as you go: Something for the body. Something for the mind. Something for the heart. Something for the spirit.

Top off your tank to avoid hitting bottom, sputtering on fumes, and collapsing on empty in a heap at the side of the road. ᛩ

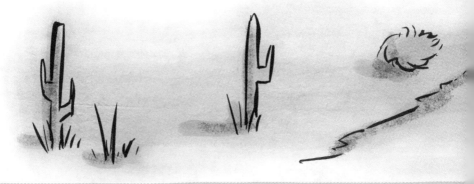

I look forward to my noon-hour runs and feel cheated if I have to cancel because of a meeting. My two- or three-hour run on Sunday is a great chance to concentrate on a single problem or just enjoy life awhile. If I feel stressed, frustrated, tired, or need a break, I'll walk around the building or through the park. The lake is my favorite reflection and renewal place: sailing or boating, going for walks, or sitting on the deck listening to the birds while I enjoy my morning cup of coffee. Ah, life is grand when you have a vision of your special place!

— Steve J.

I've learned the hard way that unrealistic expectations for my contributions to my job, family, and community ultimately lead to great loss for everyone. We're human beings, not human doings. I've learned to rest and do what I need to do to refill the well.

— Cathy V.

Giving Up or Letting Go?

To try or not to try - that is the question! A fine line can be drawn between mastery and ceaseless striving, and an even finer line between giving up and letting go. The distinction rests in action and control. Consider these four scenarios.

When you find yourself in a situation in which you have some control and you take action, you are on the road to mastery. You've chosen a strong direction and a fine destination.

When you keep pushing in a situation in which you have no control, you beat your head against the proverbial brick wall. Your ceaseless striving yields bruises and headaches.

> "There's no point in burying a hatchet if you're going to put up a marker on the site."
> – Sydney Harris

In a situation in which you have control and you do nothing, you're throwing up your hands and giving up. This action is sometimes appropriate - one can only summon the energy for so many struggles at once. However, when used as a constant pattern, you run the risk of bouncing around at the whim of the world.

When you have no control over an outcome or decision and you stop trying to push, shove and conquer, you are letting go. It's often a wise choice in a powerless situation.

> "Notice that the moment you become unhappy is usually the moment you attempt to control another person."
> – Hugh Prather

To live, think, and work effectively, exercise your influence in the areas in which you have control. Once you've reviewed your options and done your due diligence, then make your decision and act. That's mastery!

Let go of the rest. You won't help yourself or others if you continue to fret and stew about situations that are far beyond your influence and control.

An incident happened today and it's 10:32 p.m. It's still upsetting me. I realize I can't do anything about it. The person responsible isn't even aware of how she upset me and she doesn't care. Who am I hurting? Me! This isn't going to continue.
— Sharon H.

We are each exposed to many possibilities every day. Particular directions will resonate with some people and positively change their lives. Every idea isn't for everyone. With each new idea, pause and ask yourself, 'Will this help?' If the answer isn't a resounding 'yes,' give yourself permission let it go.
— Cheryl D.

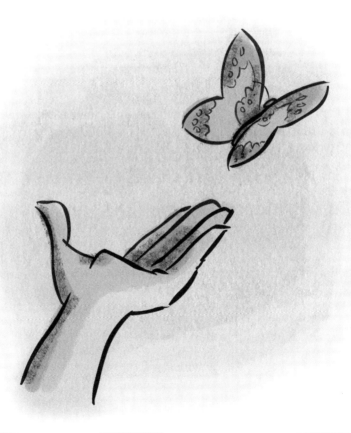

Hurting or Healing?

As I waited for my medical-test results, my mind led me down some amazing trails - most of them predicting disastrous outcomes. Within minutes, it took me from ill, to seriously ill, to languishing on my deathbed, to planning my funeral.

On what were these stories based? Nada. Zip. Nothing. No information at all! In the absence of information, my mind seemed determined to manufacture its own.

> *"You're a success every time you face down fear."*
> *— Barbara Sher*

An African tribe that teaches its children how to calm themselves in anxious situations offers a wonderful strategy to handle the pressure of the unknown. Little ones who start imagining the worst (man-eating tigers lurking at the edge of the path) spin their yarns based only on fear. They are told to watch for a pattern. Once they notice the pattern, they stop and label their flights of fancy as hurting stories - stories that don't have to be written.

As adults, we spin scary yarns about negative outcomes based on nothing but fear. This project is doomed. The market will dry up. My business will fail. Our relationship is dust.

Pay close attention to the churning of your mind. When you find yourself getting bent out of shape, particularly when evidence is lacking, pause. See if you can identify the pattern and the hurting story.

When you do, find another story to take its place: a positive scenario with a compelling vision of a preferred future. Write yourself a healing story.

Given a choice - and you have a choice - it's much better to have a whole lot of healing than a whole lot of hurting going on.

When I'm facing down fear, I replace the thoughts of gloom and doom with thoughts of a successful outcome. I ask myself: 'What will success look like in this case? What will it feel like?' Instead of visualizing disaster, I visualize everything being okay. When I think about successful outcomes, my mind and body are more calm and serene. Whatever happens, I'm better prepared to handle it – mentally, physically, and spiritually.

– Marg F.

At the beginning of a new school year, I set a goal to approach everything in a positive way. It took me months to develop this new habit. I had to learn to identify the things I really liked and wanted, take notice of them, and then verbalize them to others. I started to take fewer things for granted. Students responded and were more willing to take risks. As a leader, appreciating the talents and efforts of those around me helped me establish strong bonds with my staff.

– Frans L.

"One Of" or Repeat?

In the same eventful week, my parents celebrated their golden wedding anniversary, my eldest daughter moved out of our home, and a good friend launched her first book.

All three events were significant and presented opportunities to mark their importance. The golden wedding anniversary called for gifts and a special lunch. My daughter's departure called for one last heart-to-heart discussion, a helping hand with packing, and a farewell photo. My friend's book launch called for my attendance and sincere good wishes.

> "Begin doing what you want to do now. We have only this moment, sparkling like a star in our hand – and melting like a snowflake."
>
> – Marie Beyon Ray

This last event presented a challenge because I was already booked to attend a board meeting that same evening. I discussed my conflict with the board chair; he noted that board meetings are a monthly occurrence while the launch of a friend's first book is a "one of" event. It's a unique way of looking at tugs on your time and heart when they go head to head against each other.

Experiences that are unlikely to be repeated now take precedence over ongoing, everyday matters for me. I think you can easily recognize major life events (promotions, births, graduations, marriages, deaths) yet the smaller opportunities, though still significant, can slip by unnoticed and unmarked.

In a world of conflicting priorities, determining whether an experience is a "one of" can help you develop a sense of occasion and make a distinction. Acting on that is essential. ✿

I have come to realize that life is to be enjoyed because you only get one life and you don't know when it'll be over. Now I try not to worry about cutting the grass if I've decided to sew my current quilting project. I dedicate whole weekends to spending time with my two grandchildren. They're far more important than the housework.
— Donna G.

I was out of town at meetings when I learned a good friend had lost her father. I quickly spent the breaks rearranging my schedule so I would be home for the funeral on Wednesday. My next decision was whether to drive home in the dark on Tuesday evening or spend that evening with my mother and drive home on Wednesday morning. My friend's loss reminded me of two things — the death of my own father and that I don't spend a lot of time with Mom. The decision was easy.
— Laura S.

Racing or Dancing?

As I set up for my early morning seminar, one of the attendees arrived in a sorry state - literally shaking. I stopped my preparations to see if he was all right.

He had just navigated one of the busiest freeways in the city to get to the program. He lives in a rural area and the nonstop, high-speed, horn-honking traffic had pushed him far outside his comfort zone.

> "Some of the secret joys of living are not found by rushing from point A to point B but by inventing some imaginary letters along the way."
> – Douglas Pagels

What bothered him most was other drivers cutting in front of his vehicle. When I asked why this irritated him so much, he looked at me as though I was from Mars and exclaimed, "Because they'll get there before I do!"

The real source of his frustration was apparent. In his mind, he'd just lost a race and he was livid.

I suggested he think about freeway driving as a dance rather than a race. Someone cuts in front: presto, new partner! One driver cuts from the left and another from the right: do-si-do, you're dancing the butterfly! Tail lights flash ahead: "brake" dancer!

> "The question is not what you look at but what you see."
> – Thoreau

In truth, whether he raced or danced, the trip would have taken the same amount of time. However, his state of mind on arrival would have been completely different. He would have been present to a more positive aspect of the experience.

Instead of having run the Indy 500 and lost, he would have danced all the way to the conference room and been entertained along the way. Sometimes the pressure is all in our minds! 🌀

Being stressed about speed is a choice. When I sit in traffic, I stretch and do some mini-yoga exercises to slow down my breathing and my life. When I'm standing in line, I do isometrics – tensing and relaxing muscles without anyone knowing. I find the tension that others choose to live with funny and a bit sad. Life is too short for tension. We need to make exercise and relaxation the new thing to do!

— Marg F.

When I'm able to talk on the phone and get dinner in the oven at the same time, I think: Great! I've killed two birds with one stone. The problem is that I was never really present to enjoy or pay attention to either task at hand.

— Margot P.

Mired or Motivated?

I have more ideas than I could hope to accomplish in ten lifetimes. Although it's exciting to have options, it's also overwhelming. Where do I start? What do I do now? What do I abandon or peg as a good idea for later? Maybe you can relate.

> "You can't wring your hands and roll up your sleeves at the same time."
> – Pat Schroeder

A friend and colleague has been serving as my informal business coach. I'm full of imagination and possibilities while she brings an analytical point of view to the conversation. We've met several times to look at where I want to go with my business and how I intend to get there.

The biggest gift from those conversations is that I have narrowed my focus and prioritized my tasks. I still get bogged down, of course. I still get distracted by flights of fancy and "great" new ideas. But I have a plan to which I return, and that brings me back to earth - where progress is measured one step at a time.

> "If you wait until you have the perfect vision, you will never act. Too many forget the power of a flexible but focused alignment. Don't expect any plan to have a totally clear vision. Instead, settle for 10 to 15 degrees of focus and keep moving."
> – Jerry Paulson

The next time you find yourself swamped by possibilities, try this approach to focus your efforts. List the possibilities. Rank each one on a scale of 1 (low) to 5 (high) for each of these three criteria:

- What's the potential impact on your goals?
- How easy will it be for you to implement?
- How great is your enthusiasm for the initiative?

Dig into a few of your top-ranking items and see where they take you. High-leverage, quick-win tasks for which you are "juiced" will more likely jumpstart your engine for the long haul.

I've been reflecting on the nature of containment. Right now my life has too many possibilities for what I want to do and be. I can see so many opportunities! Daily, I pick up the tiny, beautiful, pottery inch pots on my desk and remind myself that my exuberance must be contained for me to live healthily.

— Catherine B.

Sometimes action, any action, is necessary. Too much thinking and deliberating can leave you mired in a permanent state of indecision. Sometimes even the wrong decision can be better than no decision at all. We learn from our mistakes.

— Carla P.G.

Save or Savor?

As I shared my excitement about a new book describing sewing shortcuts for the working woman, a friend - whose joy in life centers around sewing - listened patiently. At the end of my enthusiastic book review, she smiled and said, "I'm sure you'll get a lot of mileage out of this book. But I love to sew. Why would I want to make it go faster?"

> "I awake each morning torn between a desire to save the world and a desire to savor the world. This makes it hard to plan my day."
> – E. B. White

I can't say I appreciated her comment at the time. But I do now! She posed an insightful question and made an important point. We have options. Option A: rush, sprint, speed, charge, tear, race, attack. Option B: amble, mosey, saunter, stroll, roam, wander, meander. The question is: what's most appropriate to the situation and what's most likely to feed your soul and renew your spirit?

Yes, there's a time to be concerned about speed and efficiency and, yes, there's a time to simply appreciate participating in the process.

That's why it's helpful to be patient with a young colleague you are mentoring, even when you know you could handle the task in half the time. That's why it makes no sense to speed read a work of fiction you've picked up for recreational reading. That's why I golf without keeping score - so I can enjoy the outdoors and the socializing. That's why I've got an embroidery sampler I've been stitching, off and on, for almost 20 years.

I'm determined to enjoy the process of certain activities and not feel compelled to complete them simply for the sake of reaching the end.

Life's pleasures are much more than items to check off our endless lists!

Folks have told me that when I'm knitting, if I hold the needles this way or that way I'll be able knit faster, better. My objective isn't better and faster but rather more enjoyment and a challenge that's different from my daily tasks. It's the process – the journey – not the destination. What am I going to do when I get there, wherever there is? Sit on the beach?

— Brian G.

We have a beautiful park in the center of our city. I often plan five extra minutes to drive through the park and around the lake to get to my next appointment. No matter how hurried, busy, worried, or frantic I feel, that five-minute detour through the park puts me back on track with renewed energy, a positive attitude, and a smile to cap it off.

— Kathleen S.

I don't have a dishwasher and washing dishes isn't my favorite activity. Sometimes I wash them slowly. I look at each piece as I wash it and appreciate the sparkling look of the dishes when they're done. That work becomes a meditation and changes my whole experience.

— Helen W.

Yes, No, or Middle Ground?

Will you? Would you? Can you? Could you? On those short questions hang the hooks of overcommitment. Will you take on this project? Would you look after the kids for the weekend? Could you chair this committee?

The trap lies in believing there's only a yes or no answer to each question.

Say "yes" and when you realize you don't have time for the task or that it's not a fit with your interests or priorities, you reward yourself with resentment. Say "no" and when you suffer second thoughts about the wisdom of your decision or its possible effect on your relationships or future, you reward yourself with guilt.

> "Resentment is an extremely bitter diet, and eventually poisonous. I have no desire to make my own toxins."
> – Neil Kinnock

People often overlook the possibility of middle ground. Maybe you would feel comfortable taking on the project if you could shift other deadlines. Maybe you would take the kids on Friday or Saturday night but not for the whole weekend. Maybe you won't chair the committee, but you would help recruit someone who will.

The search for middle ground starts with a time out. By stepping back from the request, thinking about the impact, looking at your priorities and schedules, you may be able to find one option or several that aren't based on guilt or resentment. Look for commitments you can make with a willing heart. Find ways you can help and still be "sustainably" productive over the long haul.

Middle ground runs wide and deep. It's rich with possibilities for reasonable loads and healthy relationships.

The year I was president of two organizations was frustrating. Both held their monthly board meetings on the same Tuesday – one from 4:00 to 6:00 p.m. and the other starting at 7:00 p.m. When my traveling husband was in town, the tight schedule was not too much of a problem. However one day when my husband couldn't be home, I had to arrange for one babysitter to pick up my daughter from another babysitter, take her home, and stay with her until I could get home about 10:00 p.m. At that point, I found the backbone to say 'no' to some of the requests that came my way.

— Debby C.

When I'm asked for something that requires my time, I simply say, 'I want to think about it. I'll get back to you.' This gives me time to recover from the shock of another request and see if it fits in my calendar. I wear the idea awhile, see what it feels like, see which way I lean, and make a decision. When I say 'yes,' I really mean it!

— Denise N.

Answers Are Inside

In the early years of my business, I received an invitation for a ten-day, ten-city seminar tour. It was a tempting offer.

I spent several hours on the phone quizzing colleagues about their experiences and asking for their advice. Should I accept? Should I decline? Toward the end of my quest for insight, a wise colleague observed that I already had all the information. She suggested I needed to be quiet with myself. Then I'd know what to do.

> "There is a wisdom of the head, and a wisdom of the heart."
> – Charles Dickens

She was right. I had been busy, busy, busy gathering evidence to support what I already knew intuitively in my gut: This engagement wasn't a good fit for me.

It's possible to find plenty of good information and useful questions out there. The real gems are buried in our own hearts and minds. The toughest part is to be still and quiet enough to hear our own words of wisdom.

The next time you face a confusing challenge, grab a sheet of paper and a pen. Take ten minutes in a quiet spot. Write yourself a letter advising your best course of action.

> "Knowledge comes, but wisdom lingers."
> – Lord Alfred Tennyson

If you can silence your critical, confusing, chaotic self-talk long enough to tune into your wisest voice of sanity, you'll find that it's been there all along. You probably already know what you need to stop, start, or continue. Listen with care and be thankful for that inner voice of wisdom.

My friends tell me I come up with great, imaginative ideas for them when they ask but I often find it difficult to perform the same service for myself. Next time, I'll sit right down and write myself a letter!

— Helen W.

I'm a counselor. When people say, 'Did I say that?' I say, 'Yes, you did!' Often clients come in for counseling and ask for advice. I truly and wholeheartedly believe that we all have our best advice inside us. If we pause more and listen to our inner hero, our gut, our authentic selves, our instincts – our inner knowledge – we're usually bang on.

— Christine H.

I've come to the conclusion that the answers are on the inside not the outside. Guidebooks can help, but in the end, you have to find your own heart and write your own story.

— Linda E.

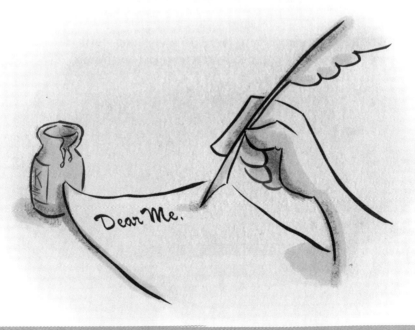

In What Order?

How much is enough? How much is too much? Negotiating reasonable workloads is challenging. In fact, concerns about "unreasonable" expectations top the list of complaints in my surveys on frustrations with time.

It's not always someone else who creates overload situations. Sometimes we are our own worst enemies. However, the expectations imposed by others can be tough to handle. You may feel reluctant to say "no" and negotiate limits, especially when it involves people in authority.

> *"You can't have it all at once and you can't have it forever. No life has room for everything in it, not on the same day."*
> *– Barbara Sher*

Your supervisor may have asked you to tackle a giant load of tasks - all within your job description, assuming you have one. However, not every team leader is skilled at determining workloads, and the expectation that anyone can accomplish everything all at once is unreasonable.

One effective way to talk about workload is to address the question, "In what order?"

Ask those sending you tasks to help you rank the relative importance of each one. Seek their advice on the order in which you need to tackle those tasks.

> *"The art of being wise is the art of knowing what to overlook."*
> *– William James*

If others continue to express confidence in your ability to handle everything at once, use the "until-further-notice" approach. List the tasks in the order you believe makes sense. Let others know your intended order of approach along with your "best guess" regarding how long each task will take.

These practices will go a long way toward helping you reset expectations to more humane and manageable levels.

A potential client asked for a proposal with an unrealistic deadline. It was extremely satisfying to confidently and diplomatically explain that, given my current commitments, I couldn't meet that deadline. The client asked me to set the deadline and we proceeded from there.

– Ruth L.

I prioritize items to complete the critical ones and take a breather when the opportunity presents itself. When I'm feeling pressured, I ask myself, 'If I don't complete this by the deadline, what will go wrong?' Then I weigh the stress against the benefit and decide if it's worth it. It's amazing how much stuff can wait a week or two.

– Sue F.

Move 'Em Out... Move On

Old files. Outdated products. Obsolete references. Unfashionable clothes. Petty grievances. Waning interests. Hopeless relationships.

Sometimes we just need to clear the clutter from our lives so we can see our way forward.

Pursuits we once enjoyed, at some point, may turn into clutter. Picture the hobbies such as photography, gardening, or biking that once consumed your interest and fueled your enthusiasm. You amassed all the tools, equipment, and supplies and there they sit - lonely, abandoned, taking up space - and inducing guilt. Once you couldn't get enough of the fun; now it feels like one more thing you should be doing.

Free stuff such as samples, magazines, and hand-me-down clothes pile up, too. Just because something is free doesn't mean you have to take advantage of the offer or hang on to it forever.

If you've outgrown it, move on. Sell the supplies or give the tools to someone who values them, but get them out of your way.

> "Getting the clutter out of your life can and will rid you of more discouragement, tiredness, and boredom than anything else you can do."
> – Don Aslett

As sad as it may be, we need to unclutter our web of relationships as well. Some relationships are more infuriating than enhancing. Peoples' needs change. Shared interests disappear. Circumstances shift. Distance grows. Appreciate those connections for the ways they enriched your life in the past. Know when it's time to move on.

In the vacuum you create, trust that new interests, new directions, and new relationships will appear. Opportunities will arise. Your enthusiasm will grow.

I eliminated a 'black cloud' today. It was the stacks of papers, file folders, and documents that crowded my work area. I took one hour to file, recycle, and forward this mountain of paper that just kept piling up. I'm looking forward to spending less time digging and searching for things.

– Lisa A.

In the mid-1990s, I sold everything and moved into a two-room hotel suite. I lived there for 18 months. I cooked my meals in a toaster oven and microwave. I learned how to play and have fun. I always had time for my friends and children. Everyone loved to come and visit. They would stay for hours because I always had time for them. They loved to be where everything was at a minimum.

– Laurie P.

Press Pause ... Press On

A farmer friend chuckles at the "helpful" truck-driving instructions offered by her husband. As she sits at the wheel maneuvering the grain truck into position, he has been known to holler, "Go ahead and back up!"

Although the instruction seems full of contradictions, I can relate to it. I regularly spend time rethinking my business - backing up for a better look at the road ahead and testing out the most promising paths to results.

> "The best way to get where we're going is to be where we are."
> – Noah benShea

Rethinking your approach to situations can be awkward and uncomfortable, like the fallout from a lesson with a golf pro. You may find yourself full of insights and ideas, jolted out of your comfortable habits, and stilted and awkward on the backswing and follow through. At times like this, pausing to rethink how your approach can bring long-term improvements can help.

The experiences of Loehr and Schwartz[9], experts in high-performance management, bear this out. They state that to perform well in any arena, we need to honor the rhythmic balance between stress and recovery - between pressing forward with all we've got and pausing for renewal and redirection.

> "We're wired up, but we're melting down."
> – Jim Loehr and Tony Schwartz

Nonstop, full-speed ahead, business-as-usual performance is rarely the best long-term strategy. It just wears us out and grinds us down.

What areas of your life might reap the benefits if you give yourself permission to "go ahead and back up"? Press pause - so you can press on with a renewed sense of direction and enthusiasm. ᘔ

A long road trip alone is the ultimate experience in quality personal time. My trip has purpose. I know where I'm heading. I'm in complete control. I know how to get there and when I'll get there. I stop when I want. I can choose quiet solitude, inspiration, information, or music. I can listen, sing, hum, whistle, or rock. Most important, I can live in the moment, enjoying free expression and total independence. It's rare to find a chunk of time in which I can get back in touch with myself. As a social person, I was surprised to discover that I enjoy my own company. The open road is my escape from a busy world. It's my time to reflect, plan, and grow. I love it!

– Kathleen S.

Speak Up

When the load is too heavy and life isn't as you wish it to be, do you ever hope that someone will read your mind and solve your problems?

As much as you might dream of a dramatic rescue, white knights on chargers are hard to come by these days. And a lot of potential white knights are having a tough time staying on their horses. The ride is just too wild.

> "Assumptions are the termites of relationships."
> – Henry Winkler

If you want a different outcome, you can't suffer in silence and hope for the best. So what do you do? Start by collecting and sharing real information about the situation. Actively negotiate options, set reasonable limits, shift deadlines, and draw on extra resources. Talk directly to people who control the situation - don't just complain to those who will commiserate, but have little or no power and influence.

> "If you want to transform the relationship, you have to have the conversation. When the conversation is real, the change occurs before the conversation is over."
> – Susan Scott

If you're the one in charge, make it "safe to say." When you react positively to those who speak their minds and hearts, people will be more direct with you. You'll hear real concerns and have access to real information - not just what others think you want to hear. This will help you make clearer assessments and better adjustments to ease the frustrations of the moment.

Together with those who "tell it like it is," you can improve the circumstances now and build more trust and capacity for the future.

The organization I work for has an insatiable appetite to consume management time. Since the organization doesn't monitor itself, I do it for the organization. I refuse to engage in all activities and meetings. I choose those that must be done or that make sense strategically.

– Alison R.

I hate bookkeeping, even though I'm an accountant! I would rather spend time with people after spending a day with numbers. I stopped doing the books for two charitable organizations and this made a difference in my life. I learned that just because I have a unique skill, I'm not obliged to give it away. I can choose to do something I like. Then both parties win.

I started gardening on weekends in the summer, sewing and playing chess on weekends in the winter, and vacationing in Fairmont! I'm much happier now.

– Marg F.

Shift Your Intentions

"You'll never meet a bunch of kinder people anywhere! They'll give you the shirts off their backs and even offer to press them for you!"

> "You create the culture around you with everything that you accept, expect, reward, and reprimand. With every action you take, every decision you make, you actually demonstrate to the people around you what is possible."
> – Lee Ann Del Carpi

"It's a dog-eat-dog world, out there! Make sure you're looking out for number one - everybody else is!"

Conflicting reports abound! Whose reality rings true? I believe each one of us plays a role in defining the nature of our workplaces, our families, and our communities. We not only discover what's out there, we influence it.

The Constructionist Principle speaks directly to this effect. Its basic idea is that life doesn't just happen to us; each of us plays a part in creating the situations we experience. We build meaning and reality through conversations and interactions.

> "Thoughts become things... choose the good ones."
> – Mike Dooley

For a quick lesson in the Constructionist Principle, scowl at someone and watch how that person responds. Then smile at someone and notice what comes back your way. Offer to lend a hand to support someone struggling with a task, then note what happens to your relationship with that person.

Watch closely over the next few days to see how your expectations, your actions, and your reactions contribute to your everyday experience of life, both at work and at home.

Then pay close attention to your intentions. Focus on the things you would like more of in your life. Lay the foundation and watch what grows.

Every morning I look in the mirror – if I can smile at myself, or even laugh, it's going to be a good day. If I can't smile, it's time to go back to bed! Have you ever spoken to someone on the phone who is smiling while they talk to you? Even a bright, cheery voice over the phone can lighten one's step!

– Gregg H.

When managers confront workplace bullies, they often focus on termination or discipline. If we focused on having a respectful workplace and not allowing other kinds of behavior, the results would be better. I often find myself asking what is the intention!

– Kathy D.

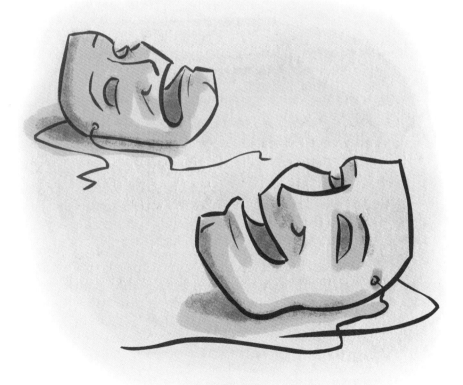

"Unwhelm" Yourself

It's no surprise that one of the top-ranking complaints in today's world is feeling overwhelmed. You may be familiar with the word and the drowning feeling yourself!

Dig into the root of any word and you can find new ways to look at a situation. The word overwhelmed comes from the root word whelmed, which means to turn over, cover up, bury, or submerge.

> "We have surrounded ourselves with time-saving technological gadgetry, only to be overwhelmed by plans that cannot be carried out, appointments that cannot be honored, schedules that cannot be fulfilled, and deadlines that cannot be met."
>
> – Jacob Needleman

When demands on you are too much, it feels as though you're being smothered or buried alive. With no access to the big picture (sight blurred and horizon gone), you lose any sense of direction and perspective. You don't know which way is up or out. The fact that you're fighting for air makes the struggle that much tougher.

So the next time you feel whelmed - or worse, overwhelmed - take two actions.

First, catch your breath. Literally. Find fresh air. Take a deep breath. Still your mind and fill your lungs. Calm your racing heart. Cool off. Settle down.

Second, get your bearings. Step away from the problem. Back up for a wider view of the whole situation. Put the demands in context. Get a bead on the pressures and scan your options.

These two actions - catching your breath and getting your bearings - will help you find a smoother path through each pressure-filled situation. Think of it as drown-proofing for the 21st century.

We were moving back into our house after having had the hardwood floors refinished. My partner and I were moving the fridge back in place after midnight (our first mistake) and I conceded to his plan, although I didn't think it was well thought out. In haste, we put a foot-long scratch in the middle of the kitchen floor. I could have lost it, but I told him we needed to take a break. I stomped around the backyard in a steaming rage. After a few minutes I thought, 'It's only a scratch; it can be fixed with one phone call to the floor guy.' Yet if I had acted irrationally against someone I love, that scratch could've taken a long time to heal. I went back in with my proposal to immediately get the scratch repaired. The floor guy was back in a few days, and the scar is invisible.

– Dani V.D.

Zap a Snit

Over the years, most of our family vacations have included an emotional meltdown by one member or another at some point during the trip. Our most "memorable" vacations have featured multiple meltdowns, triggered by lapses in communication or thwarted expectations.

One vacation meltdown occurred over something my traveling partner couldn't control. Really, what are the chances he would consciously choose to have a killer cold coupled with zero enthusiasm on our only day on the beautiful Greek island of Mykonos?

Nevertheless, there I was - stuck in a snit - actively making a rough day worse. The speaker in me tried to talk it out. The writer in me grabbed my journal and scratched out my frustrations on paper. Neither approach tempered my bad humor.

> "Gratitude unlocks the fullness of life. It turns what we have into enough, and more. It turns denial into acceptance, chaos to order, confusion to clarity. It can turn a meal into a feast, a house into a home, a stranger into a friend. Gratitude makes sense of our past, brings peace for today, and creates a vision for tomorrow."
>
> – Melody Beattie

It was only a change in my frame of reference that turned my mood around. When I switched from listing my gripes and complaints to consciously noting all the things for which I was grateful (in spite of my disappointment and selfish lack of compassion), I found it impossible to maintain a negative head of steam about the situation. I zapped the snit right out of existence.

Try this the next time a snit hangs a hammerlock on your heart. List the things for which you are grateful and appreciative. Watch your mood swing to the upbeat side of the positiv-o-meter. It's impossible to hold onto a snit and embrace gratitude at the same time.

I attend Al-Anon and have learned that I can't control everything. When my snits take hold of me, I back off. I'm learning to detach with love and take inventory of what I'm grateful for. It works.
— Jan N.

I'm becoming better at being present in the moment. When I'm not, I'm usually spinning my mental wheels in worry and recriminations. My cue to pausing and coming back to the present — and the reality of the absolute glory of this life I'm living — is negative thoughts! I use negative thoughts as a cue to help me return to stillness and joy and it's truly wonderful!
— Corinne A.

Exercise Your Options

Conference over. Sleep long. Body rested. Hot shower. Room-service breakfast. Travel day. Check schedule. Oops!

If I'm taking the airport shuttle, I have 30 minutes to dry my hair, dress, pack clothes and conference collectibles, pay the bill, check out, and get on board. I shift into serious hustle mode. My heart rate rises as the clock speeds on. Then my brain kicks in.

> "You can be the master of your universe or a poster child for the breathless society. It's your choice."
> — Dr. Patt Schwab

The shuttle leaves in less than 30 minutes. It winds through a 60-minute, multistop route to the airport. Cabs leave any time, head directly to the airport, and only take 20 minutes on a sleepy Sunday morning.

Price of shuttle? $12. Price of cab? $24. Price of sanity? The difference is just $12. Who says you can't buy time and peace of mind?

Of course, if I had started earlier, I wouldn't have suffered the surcharge for sanity! But who among us always thinks ahead and always leaves enough lead time?

> "A new idea about oneself or some aspect of one's relations to others unsettles all one's other ideas. No matter how slightly, it shifts one's entire orientation and somewhere along the line of consequences it changes one's behavior."
> — Patricia McLaughlin

When we find ourselves fraught with frenzy, it's easy to miss the options right under our noses.

Are there any crazy-making assumptions that are driving your actions these days? Take a closer look next time you find yourself running around in circles. Pause, stop chasing your tail, and scout out the choices.

Bridget came to our Toastmasters meeting last night. We hadn't seen her for almost a year. She and her family had taken the ultimate 'pause' this past year. They took one year off from all activities: Toastmasters meetings, swimming, hockey, soccer, etc. She reorganized her work schedule to be home for lunch with her kids and pick them up from school at 3:30 p.m. When they got home there was 'nothing' to do! No rushing off to numerous activities. They played cards and games. She says it was a great year. They learned a lot about each other and spent quality time together. Next year they'll return to the extracurricular activities they enjoy most. A few years down the road, they'll do it again. How many people take time off to regenerate themselves and their families?

— Rose-Marie C.

Ask The Good-News Question

On a beautiful fall day I caught a ride with a cab driver who could've taken the grand prize for the world's darkest outlook on life. In response to my comments on the freshness of the morning, the beauty of the autumn leaves, and the glassy calm of Wascana Lake, he responded in turn, "Frost last night - gonna make the harvest tough! Just reminds me winter's coming! It's never like that when I go fishing!"

I'm sure if he won $100,000 in the lottery, he wouldn't waste a minute celebrating. He would immediately launch a litany of complaints about the uselessness of a prize that small!

> "The hardest arithmetic to master is that which enables us to count our blessings."
> – Eric Hoffer

Our point of view has a lot to do with our experience of the day. It's possible to shift from pure pessimism to a more optimistic response to life. It's mostly a matter of attention. What do you notice? What do you hang onto? How do you start conversations with yourself and others?

As day's end nears and you shut down your computer, pull on your coat, or jump in the car to head home, ask yourself this simple question: "What went well today?"

Ask the same question of colleagues as you close up shop and of family members as you gather for the evening. Yes, you'll eventually get to the complaints, but at least the good news of the day will hold center stage and pride of place. That's all it takes to shift your focus. 🍃

Our family struggled to accept a serious health challenge for one of my siblings. At the same time another sibling's marriage was falling apart. My parents were so focused on the problems they became negative and lost sight of what was wonderful in the world. In a conversation with Dad, I asked him to step back and think about what he was grateful for and what was wonderful in the world, then email his thoughts to me. He emailed me the next morning and now he emails me every day to share what is great and wonderful in their world. I now have a journal with this collection that I can share. It contains many memories and important family events. It's all about all of us, as a family. I treasure this because it has been given so freely, honestly, and sincerely. My parents believe this commitment to share the positive has changed their lives.

– Myrna B.

It Is What It Is

A Virginia Creeper vine runs up the south wall of our house. In May, you'll find it full of springtime enthusiasm - new growth and bright-green tendrils reaching in every direction. Through June and July, the heat, aphids, and grasshoppers all take a run at it. By the end of August, it resembles the end of summer - worn out and tired.

By that time, there's no point in arguing, pushing back, resisting, or trying to coax the creeper back to robust health. The leaves are about to turn red, dry up, and fall to the ground. All the watering, fertilizing, and gardening skills you can summon will get you nowhere. Fall has rounded the corner and is knocking on the door.

In the words of a tell-it-like-it-is television personality, "It is what it is!"

What a useful phrase this can be: It is what it is! In some situations all the fighting, tinkering, and resisting in the world won't change a thing or make everything right.

> "The truth will set you free but first it will make you miserable."
> – Jim Davis

"Maybe the stock market will pick up." "I'd like to be young again." "I'd give anything to take back those words." "I wish I hadn't been in this accident." "I can make this perfect." Well, the stock market will do what it will do. The years have flown by. The words have been spoken. The accident is a fact of life. Some things are flawed.

It is what it is! The challenge is to pause long enough to accept the facts of a situation, choose a healthy response, and appreciate what's right in front of us - despite its frail, sad, imperfect, or weary condition. ✑

I've never wished to be somewhere else in my life. When my children were small, that was the best place to be. When they left home to be on their own and left Dad and me alone, that was really good! Now, when they're getting married and bringing grandchildren home to visit, that's the best that can be. Isn't change great?

— Donna G.

Whenever a friend forwards an email message that I suspect contains incorrect information, I feel compelled to search out the correct information and forward it back to my friend. I'm going to give up my compulsion to correct things, including pointing out editing errors in the daily paper! I realize I'm wasting precious hours feeding my perfection plague.

— Jean F.

Give to Live

When life grows busy, do you find yourself cutting back on your offers to extend a helping hand? If so, that could be a short-sighted strategy.

A study conducted for the National Institutes of Health[10] found that contributing to the lives of others may help us extend our own.

In the five-year study of 423 older couples, researchers found that people who reported helping others reduced their risk of dying by almost 60 percent - compared to those in the study who gave neither practical help nor emotional support to family, friends, and neighbors.

> "Too often we underestimate the power of a touch, a smile, a kind word, a listening ear, an honest compliment, or the smallest act of caring, all of which have the potential to turn a life around."
> – Leo Buscaglia

For women, the act of reaching out to offer support is even more important. Researchers Klein and Taylor[11] found that the hormone oxytocin, which women's bodies release as a response to stress, encourages women in "tending and befriending" behaviors. For women, the act of gathering with and caring for others has a positive, calming effect.

> "Sometimes someone says something really small and it just fits right into this empty place in your heart."
> – Angela Chase

What is the active status of your "giving spirit" - alive and well or ailing and failing? Could you take a minute to offer a word of encouragement to the downhearted colleague one desk over? Could you take five minutes to call your elderly relative and see how she's doing? Could you take ten minutes to shovel a walk for the neighbor next door?

Small gestures - big returns. Give strong - live long.

My neighbor is 93. Yesterday morning when we went for coffee, he asked, 'Are you going into Redwater?' It's a town about 10 miles from here. I said, 'I could be.' He had something to pick up at the post office. Sure, it carved some time out of my hectic week but so what? If we're too busy to spend time with people in our lives, we're too busy. When my dad passed away, my mom needed help on an ongoing basis. I cherish each moment I spent with her before she passed away. Life is short. Invest your time in the lives of those you love and in action for those you would serve.

– Bob H.

Move Things Forward

Many of my mornings begin with a walk along the beautiful South Saskatchewan River valley, just two blocks from home. My route winds past a giant boulder on the bank. It's the perfect perch for a moment's rest and meditation.

> "Resentment is like taking poison and waiting for the other person to die."
> – Malachy McCourt

I recently headed out on my morning stroll, anticipating a peaceful journey. As I turned the corner and headed toward the river, I discovered that some aspiring street artist had selected our fence as a perfect canvas. We'd been tagged and I was furious! Now I needed that walk more than ever.

> "Life is a lot simpler than we make it."
> – Cheryl Dougan

I arrived at the river - still smoldering over the graffiti - only to make a second discovery. "My" rock had also been hit by a crew of performance artists. Broken beer bottles were their media of choice. So much for the peace of the morning. Now I was really ticked off! The nerve! The disrespect!

After two days of intermittent fuming, it finally occurred to me that I could choose another response. I didn't have to remain a victim - stuck in blame and fury. I could do something to move things forward. I grabbed the sandpaper, dustpan, and broom. In less than an hour, I'd cleaned up both messes and made something right in the world. My two days of needless smoldering had wasted far more than one hour's energy.

> "The guy's behaving like a jerk. How much power are you going to give him over your life?"
> – Tristan Katz

We have options in every arena of our lives. We can serve up Misery Stew, wallowing in anger, frustration, and despair over the careless actions of others; or we can channel that energy into more creative solutions and get on with our lives. The choice is yours and mine. ෴

The sudden death of my younger brother led to a great deal of soul searching about what family means to me and how I could use this tragedy toward a positive experience. I needed more time outside of work for me and my family. I approached my supervisor with a proposal to take a cut in pay and take off one day every week. With the support of a forward-thinking supervisor, fellow staff, and the owners, I've been living this arrangement for three years. I don't even think about the money anymore. It's been replaced with time spent in my daughter's classroom, getting back to my sewing machine, and stealing a few moments to relax and read! Sometimes we just have to ask and be prepared to act.

— Kathleen F.D.

Reset Your Mindset

In an instant, the flight flipped from calm to out of control. Lift ... roll ... slam! Lift ... roll ... slam! White knuckles and green faces surfaced all around me. The flight attendant dropped to her seat and strapped herself in without announcement. The passengers fell silent - with three notable exceptions.

Three little cowgirls, accompanied by their long, tall cowboy dad, were seated at the rear of the plane. They were about seven, five, and three years old - cute as could be in their Western skirts, vests, and red gingham shirts. With white straw hats on their heads and red vinyl boots on their feet, they were all set for their first plane ride.

In contrast to the fear-filled adults, the enthusiastic cowgirl trio punctuated every slam of the plane with giggles of glee and a high-pitched chorus of "Wheeeeeeeeeeeeeee!"

After a dozen wild lifts, rolls, and slams, one little voice hollered in obvious delight, "Daddy! You told us this was gonna be fun. But you didn't say it was gonna be this much fun!"

> "All misery begins in the mind, fueled by the stories we tell ourselves about what should have happened, what ought to happen."
> – Dr. Christiane Northrup

The three little cowgirls had no idea how a flight should unfold. Because they had no expectations, they simply relaxed and enjoyed the adventure. They taught me a thing or two that day.

Sometimes a plan for what ought to happen turns into a liability - especially if that plan keeps you from appreciating what actually shows up in your life. Don't let the picture of your preferred future keep you from enjoying a less-than-perfect present. Take advantage of every opportunity to reset your mindset.

I'm no longer waiting! I no longer promise myself, 'I'll be happy when ...' or 'I'll take a break when ...' I'm learning to live in the moment and consciously trying to enjoy everything I do. I know that my inbox will always be full and I'm learning to deal with that. In the meantime, I realize this is my life and it's to be enjoyed. Whether I'm doing dishes or checking my email, I live that moment to the fullest. If I keep waiting to be happy until my house is clean and fully renovated or until I get my budget organized, I'll be waiting until I'm dead!

— Jennifer G.

Celebrate Yourself

When I bought myself a bunch of flowers, the florist asked if I wanted a gift card to go with them. I declined, saying they were just for me.

"All the more reason to add a card," she declared. "I always write myself a card when I buy myself flowers."

When I asked what she wrote, she replied, "Well, it depends on the day. Sometimes it's: 'Thanks for being you.' Other times it's: 'Wow! You're smart and gorgeous, too!'"

We shared a chuckle. I left with the flowers and a card in hand.

> "Plant your own garden and decorate your own soul, instead of waiting for someone to bring you flowers."
> – Veronica A. Shoffstall

It was a simple reminder of an important lesson. The florist knows how to fill her own wellspring of appreciation. With her own spirits freshly topped up, she's in a much better position to share her goodwill with others.

Do you take yourself for granted too often? I do. If we don't show ourselves some positive attention from time to time, who will? Most of us don't have our loving mothers following us around moment by moment, applauding our courage, cheering our sense of adventure, or delighting in our presence. This is true in our work and personal lives. And if it's true for us, it's true for others as well.

> "The way you treat yourself sets the standard for others."
> – Sonya Friedman

What would life be like if you extended a bit more appreciation in your own direction more often? What would it be like if you encouraged others to do the same?

What would you write on your card today? ༄

I have a 'feeling good' list posted on my fridge, especially for down days. It lists things that pick up my spirits such as take a bubble bath and curl up with a good book in front of the fireplace. When I notice my spirits are low, I pick something from my list and do it. It helps!

– Sheila F.

I was completely snowed under with work and papers due for classes. What did I do? I signed up for flamenco dancing classes – two and a half hours a night! Amazingly, it made it easier to do everything because I was doing something fun, creative, and energetic.

– Geri B.

We Are They

In an earlier career as a camp counselor, I woke up one morning whacking myself on the head. I'd fallen asleep with my hand tucked under my pillow and cut off the circulation in my arm.

In my sleepy stupor, I was vaguely aware of a weight sitting on my head. Assuming that it was a bat (since they frequently took a swing through the cabins), I flailed at it with my "dead" arm. With the "bat" apparently jumping and dancing on my head, I increased the tempo of my swatting, which multiplied the effect. I finally beat the feeling back into my arm and realized to my embarrassment that I was doing this to myself.

> "Yelling someone to rest, to stop doing, while you are racing by and doing more is not effective."
> — Oriah Mountain Dancer

These days, our pace is such that our senses are often numbed. Short on sleep and long on ambition, we work ourselves to exhaustion. We file our feelings and shelve our hungers for more convenient times. In short, we do it to ourselves - day after day!

Individually and collectively, we create the culture that adds to the pressure we feel. We are they! Every time we agree to an inappropriate request, reinforce behaviors that lead to burnout, or sign on for overload, we give the wheel another spin.

> "The golden rule is of no use to you whatever unless you realize it is your move."
> — Frank Crane

What are the alternatives? We could become more thoughtful about our everyday decisions. We could pause more often to tune in to our feelings and senses. We could create options that lead to a sane and satisfying pace of life. Through the collective effect of our individual choices, we can calm a world that's spinning out of control.

I'm so busy taking care of others and solving their problems, I forget what's important for me. I have the disease to please and I need to stop it. I need to quit doing, doing, doing, and enjoy just being.

– Lori B.

We work at high-stress and quickly changing jobs. We have agreed, as a group, to look after one another. This is as simple as inviting someone who's feeling snowed under to take a break.

– Lee F.

No matter how busy I am, I spend a couple of minutes reflecting on what I'm doing in the bigger picture. Pause always brings me back to my personal mission and values. If I'm into things that are congruent with my goals and values, pausing gives me an energy boost. If I'm doing something that isn't contributing, it challenges me to look at what I am doing and why!

– Gael M.

Be Here Now

Race to the shower. Race to the closet. Race to the coffee pot. Race to the car. Race to work. Race to a meeting. Race to lunch. Race to the dentist. Race back to work. Race to another meeting, then another meeting. Race to the dry cleaner. Race to the supermarket. Race home. Race through dinner. Race youngster number one to soccer practice, youngster number two to a music lesson, and yourself to a community meeting. Race home again. Collapse into bed. Wake up tomorrow and start the race all over again.

> "The moment one gives close attention to anything, even a blade of grass, it becomes a mysterious, awesome, indescribably magnificent world in itself."
> – Henry Miller

Does this sound familiar? How much of your day do you spend meeting yourself coming and going?

In the hustle and pressure of daily life, it's easy to be anywhere else but present. We find ourselves trapped in regrets about yesterday or filled with anxiety for tomorrow. Yet this place - this moment in time - is all we have. If we've missed it, then it's gone forever.

The challenge for each one of us is to be here now. Post-race and post-haste, here's a simple way to settle down and be more present. Try this: Stand or sit still for a few seconds. (Yes, you can spare ten seconds. It's your life after all.) As you breathe in, draw the word here into your mind. As you breathe out, bring the word now into your mind. Repeat three times.

> "Each moment is a place you've never been."
> – Mark Strand

Pause to check: Are you here now? Take every opportunity to shift your attention from hurry to here. ❧

Here's my trick to get into the 'now.' I stop and pay attention to what my senses are telling me: sight, sound, feel, etc. Then I stop the 'race' by taking a moment to be grateful for something. Getting in touch with my senses, in combination with a grateful thought, sends a wave of warmth over me that breaks the race-rush tension.

– Jane M.

Being still (physically, mentally, and emotionally) creates a wonderful, peaceful place that's often missing in my life. My focus is helping to create a more peaceful, healthy, and joyful world. These qualities are all accessible in my inner world if I'm willing to be still and allow them to be seen!

– David G.

Comes With The Territory

A young mother complained that her living room looked like the fallout from a toy factory explosion. When she told me she was the mother of three preschool boys, I laughed. That kind of mess comes with the territory. Short of banning toys and guaranteeing a group of unhappy children, the mess will only go away as the wee ones grow.

Frustrating? Yes. Worth ranting and raving about? No.

A lot of situations are like that in our lives - at work and at home. The challenges come with the territory.

Sign on as a career public servant? Prepare to weather the winds and storms of politics, especially in the months before and after an election. It comes with the territory.

Jump into a career as a schoolteacher? You will be taking your vacations during the busiest travel seasons of the year. It comes with the territory.

> "Build a bridge and get on over it."
> – Edward Walker

Add a newborn to your family? Welcome to sleep deprivation and messy confusion. It comes with the territory.

When we waste time and energy wailing and railing against the basic nature of our chosen arenas, we send the reading on our stress-o-meters through the roof.

It's best to stop fighting and accept the fallout of our circumstances. Or if the pinch in values and fit grows unbearable, it may be time to seek out a different arena. 🌀

Constant interruptions are part of my job. However, I find it frustrating when the interruptions result from technical difficulties. How dare the printer stop working now? How dare my car have a flat tire now? I have to force myself to admit that there could've been a worse time for the flat tire!

— Jocelyn F.

Since the arrival of my first grandchild, I no longer worry about things that used to seem so important. I can't get back the time with my own children that I lost because I was so busy dusting and cooking. I realize how short our time here is. I treasure every moment I have with her. This includes all the sticky fingerprints that I was always in a rush to wash away. If you're a young parent, enjoy those precious first years, the elementary school functions, and all the excitement and hardships of raising teenagers, because they're gone before you know it.

— Sharon H.

Dive Deep

I often find myself confronting two intriguing questions. They're the kind that bring me up short and won't let me get away with glib and shallow answers.

The first pops into my mind in the midst of tedious and seemingly pointless tasks. It asks: "How much of my life do I want to spend doing this?"

Its partner shows up when I find myself stuck in a frustrating emotional swamp. The question: "How much of my life do I want to spend feeling like this?"

Perhaps it has to do with reaching mid-life. Maybe it has to do with drawing closer to my mortality or realizing that I don't have forever. I don't know.

I find myself questioning where I spend my time and how I spend my energy. I'm being much more thoughtful in my answers and discerning in my choices.

Am I making the most of my talents and abilities? Am I doing more of those things for which I am most uniquely suited? Am I acting in superficial ways or am I living from the depth of my truth and experience? Whoa! Big issues! Deep questions! Scary territory! Important stuff!

> "What I focus on in life is what I get. If I concentrate on how bad, wrong, or inadequate I am, on what I can't do and how there's not enough time to do it, isn't that what I get every time? And when I think about how powerful I am, what I have to contribute, and the difference I can make, then that's what I get. You see, I recognize that it's not what happens to you; it's what you do about it."
> – W. Mitchell

Try addressing these questions and see where they take you. How much of the rest of your life do you want to spend doing X or feeling Y? The answers might confirm you're on the right track or point you in the direction of new, uncharted territory.

I spent many years as a working mother and a perpetual pleaser. After being ill, I realized I may not have many more chances to do the things I've been waiting to do. I now let the dust balls accumulate for a few days. We eat more Sunday dinners in the kitchen with place mats instead of a linen tablecloth. I have a little dog I absolutely love and I take her for walks. I go to the gym. I sit on the patio. I love to work in the garden, even though I have a brown thumb! I read lots of books. I have lunch with friends and go to movies. Sometimes I just sit, reflect, and enjoy the day or do nothing at all. If I don't get the floor polished or the beds made and if we have pizza for supper once in a while, the world doesn't stop and nobody cares.

— Barb C.

Find Hidden Value

On the day before Halloween, the pumpkin pickings at the supermarket were pretty slim. We ended up with two lopsided, lumpy, strange jack-o-lanterns-to-be.

An amazing thing happened when we sat down to carve. Our bulging, tilting, less-than-perfect raw materials forced us to think differently. To carve any face at all, we had to take ourselves off automatic, pause, and rethink everything.

How could we open these things up? Where would we place the eyes, the nose, the mouth? How would we handle a shape that seemed inclined to tip and roll across the table?

In the end, both jacks turned out great - unusual, unique, and engaging. They were truly original works of art.

> "Until we can embrace our lives wholeheartedly, aware of our limitations and committed to making the most of our unique circumstances and gifts, we haven't fully accepted ourselves for the people we are or fully forgiven ourselves for the people we aren't."
>
> – Kent Nerburn

Every day and every person carry that same potential. It's easy to write off a rainy day as a waste or forget that someone's individual quirkiness adds flavor, intrigue, and interest to our world.

Our challenge is to take a closer look at our situations and at those around us - that employee, child, or face in the mirror - all less than perfect, but each one ripe with hidden value and possibilities. Having glimpsed what lies below, can we find ways to appreciate more of who we are and where we're going every single day?

Too many of us wait for the weekend or vacation to rejuvenate, relax, replenish, and refresh. We don't see the opportunities of the day. I try to feed my soul throughout the day. The moments come in work and in relaxation. The sun shines on a sink full of dishes and clean, soapy water. The house is clean, the fridge is full, the laundry is done — and I'm home alone! The lights dim and the movie is about to start. I drive into the country on a clear night, spread a blanket, and watch the stars. I sit on the deck with my coffee on the first, warm spring morning.

— Charlotte M.

In Lieu of Flowers

I don't make it a practice to read the daily obituaries in the newspaper. However, recently I read a stranger's obituary all the way to the end. I didn't know the woman but something about the challenging expression I saw in her photo drew me into her story.

She had packed a lot of living into her 47 years: two marriages, two children, a granddaughter, camping, fishing, boating, gardening, canning, singing, dancing, and a career in health care.

> "We're in such a hurry most of the time, we never get much of a chance to talk. The result is a kind of day-to-day shallowness, a monotony that leaves a person wondering years later where all the time went and sorry that it's all gone."
> – Robert M. Pirsig

But it was the message near the end of her life story that brought me up short. It read: "In lieu of flowers we ask that you please spend some special time with your families, friends, and loved ones. They are what really matter."

It's one of the most powerful calls to action I've ever seen. That compelling message energized my weekend plans for connecting

with my extended family. I arranged a visit with my parents at the farm. I dropped in to see an elderly aunt and called another. And I made time to listen - to really listen - to those closest to me who live in my very own home.

What about you? Have you delayed any visits, calls, or connections because you think you have all the time in the world? Right now just might be the best time in the world!

> I ran into my sister's boyfriend at the corner store. I said a quick hello and mentioned I was in a hurry and that I'd stop to talk next time. He and a friend were picking up junk food for a drive to their cabin. They got to the lake later that evening. The cabin is on the far side. They normally canoe from the near shore to the cabin. A storm came up during the crossing and swamped the canoe. Both boys died. I never got a 'next time.' It makes me think twice about passing up opportunities to spend time with a friend. I still don't stop every time, but I certainly consider the potential that every encounter could be a last encounter."
>
> – Fred H.

Lift Up Your Eyes

The motto of the University of Calgary (where I studied for my master's degree in continuing education) is "Mo shuiles togam suas." It's a Gaelic phrase taken from one of the psalms. Translated, it means: "I will lift up my eyes." What an inspired call to action!

My seminar participants tell me their overloaded days are often spent with their heads down - not eyes up. With their noses to the grindstone preoccupied with tasks and details, they wade their way through each day's responsibilities, always fretting about the details.

> "If you must live an unexamined life, please don't inflict it on others."
> – Parker J. Palmer

If that's true for you, try shifting that practice just a smidge. As you move through your day, take a moment here and there to lift up your eyes. Step out of the car - lift up your eyes. Step out of a meeting - lift up your eyes. Tune in to the bigger picture and the reason you are about to pursue the tasks at hand. You'll find a broader, higher, deeper purpose.

Real estate agents aren't just brokering cash and property; they're helping people make a home. Nurses aren't just checking blood pressure; they're helping someone live a long and healthy life. I'm not just writing tips and sharing tools; I'm helping people find perspective and experience peace of mind.

Research in time-management effectiveness shows that the more clear individuals and organizations are about their purposes, the easier it is for them to focus on their priorities. The greatest returns lie in wrestling down the answers to those big, important, underlying questions of values and direction.

What larger purpose do you see when you pause to lift up your eyes?

People want easy tips on how to better organize their work or home lives. As a result, day planners and systems become the focus. Sometimes what they really need is to reflect on the real priorities and 'why.' If you clarify values, you can clean up your to-do list. Yet more people will seek the help of a to-do technician than a values coach.

— Doug G.

I take time to pause during the day by purposely watching my screensaver on my computer for a few minutes. I have photos of my family on it. This reminds me of my priorities in my life and helps me focus on what's important.

— Lisa T.

Bless the Stress

Stop for a moment. Look around at the array of options and choices in our modern world. Hundreds of television programs are available at the click of a button. Thousands of items from around the world are for sale at your neighborhood shopping center or on the Internet. Travel agents highlight a deal a day for perfect get-away destinations. Sales people in every marketplace - insurance, automobiles, furniture - offer more service and product options than you could hope to review in a lifetime. Ways of communicating with family, friends, and colleagues that didn't exist a decade ago are now available at speeds that we could never have imagined.

> "The fact that some choice is good doesn't necessarily mean that more choice is better."
> — Barry Schwartz

With all this, it's easy to lose track of one basic point: Issues about which opportunity to pursue or which gadget to buy are questions of privilege.

In many places in this world, the pressing question of the day isn't how to fit the grocery shopping between the company barbecue and the youngster's soccer game, but whether your family will have any food on the table tonight. Some people aren't worried about how to handle an outrageous number of email messages; they're concerned they've had no news from friends and family trapped in a war zone half a world away. Some people aren't frazzled about making it to work on time through heavy traffic, they're wondering whether they'll make it home at all through the gunfire and suicide bombers.

> "When I hear someone sigh, 'Life is hard,' I am always tempted to ask, 'Compared to what?'"
> — Sydney Harris

That's not to suggest that our daily challenges and difficulties don't matter. Rather, let's acknowledge their relative importance and put them into perspective. In many ways in our modern world, stressed is blessed!

Listening to the news or reading it makes me thankful that my life is, well, so dull. I'm thankful that I've never seen a natural disaster. I'm thankful my children are healthy. I'm thankful I can wake up each day and make a difference somewhere just by being a decent person. It's useful to be aware. It makes us more tolerant and thankful.
— Vera T.

I had a big meeting with a new client and I was late, but I relaxed and said to myself that I would get there when I got there. I walked up to the building 15 minutes late, just as the firefighters were allowing everyone back into the building! I was right on time.
— Sheryl M.

What Next?

What do you see yourself doing three years from now? It's the kind of question one might ponder over a glass of wine by the fire on a long winter's night. But if it's a good question, why save it for dark and melancholy moments? For that matter, why limit it to three years?

Over the years I've created several lists of things I'd like to do in my lifetime. I've clipped pictures and phrases from magazines, assembling collages of my future. I still look at them: "Fit for life. Blessings of friends. Loved and in love for a lifetime." Pictures of people and places, including the rolling hills of Tuscany, the white domes of Santorini, and a gondola floating down the Grand Canal in Venice. We recently vacationed in the Mediterranean, fulfilling dream number 45 and capturing our own pictures and memories.

> "What's important is simple. Know what you value and invest your time accordingly. This is integrity and it will bring you peace."
> – Roberta Shaler

These desires aren't specific in the way of goals and resolutions. They have no dates, no timelines, and no formal plans attached. However, these intentions give form to our wishes and open the door to the longings of our lives. And they work!

What are your intentions for the next few years of your life? Watch and listen for the images, words, and phrases that catch your eye and call your name. Clues to the puzzle are everywhere. Collect them and piece them all together. Pause to build the future of your dreams and think about your larger purpose. As my colleague Ian Percy states, "... the absence of purpose is what makes people frantic and desperate for some form of rescue."

Let yourself dream. I've learned that rational thought and analysis will only get you so far down this path of inquiry. Gut feeling, instinct, and the longings of the heart tell the rest of the story.

I review and update my wish list on my birthday. I highlight those things I've accomplished. I strike through any items that no longer appeal. I add to the list. I believe it helps set the direction for the important 'to do' items in my life and helps me reflect on my blessings. This has become a positive annual practice for me.

– Kim B.

Years ago, when my brother graduated from college, he had two choices: begin work immediately or take the summer off and go to Europe with his buddies. He called me for advice. I asked him how old he was. 'Twenty,' he said. 'Well,' I said, 'let's say you work until you're 65 years old. If you begin working right now, you'll work for 45 years. If you go to Europe, you'll work for 44 years and 10 months.' He went to Europe.

– Jeff R.

Endnotes

[1] "Don't Manage Time, Manage Yourself," *Fast Company*, D. Beardley, April/May 1998.

[2] "Are Vacations Good for Your Health?" *Psychosomatic Medicine*, B. Gump & K. Matthews, Sept/Oct 2000, 62:608-612.

[3] "Beware The Busy Manager," *Harvard Business Review*, H. Bruch & S. Goshal, February 2002, pp. 62-69.

[4] "Driving Meditation," *Present Moment, Wonderful Moment: Mindfulness Verses for Daily Living*, T. Hahn, Parallax Press, 1990.

[5] Excerpt from "Johnny Johnson's Wedding (Sons of Knute – Christmas)" © Garrison Keillor 1983. Reprinted with permission from Garrison Keillor, Prairie Home Productions, LLC.

[6] *Margin: How To Create The Emotional, Physical, Financial & Time Reserves You Need*, R. Swenson, NavPress, 1992.

[7] "IT Rage: We All Know The Feeling," *The Star Phoenix*, February 9, 2002, p. F16.

[8] *The Artist's Way: A Spiritual Path To Higher Creativity*, J. Cameron, Tarcher/Putnam, 1992.

[9] *The Power of Full Engagement: Managing Energy, Not Time, Is the Key to High Performance and Personal Renewal*, J. Loehr & T. Schwartz, The Free Press, 2003.

[10] "Providing Social Support May Be More Beneficial Than Receiving It," *Psychological Science*, S. L. Brown et al., Volume 14 Issue 4, July 2003, p. 320.

[11] "Female Responses to Stress: Tend and Befriend, Not Fight or Flight," *Psychological Review*, Taylor, S. E. et al, (2000) 107(3), p 411-429.

Books ... And More Books ...

For more information and inspiration on work-life balance and renewal, check out some of my favorite references.

Bascobert Kelm, J. (2005). *Appreciative Living: The Principles of Appreciative Inquiry in Personal Life*. Wake Forest: Venet Publishers. A guide to creating and appreciating what you want most in life.

Borysenko, J. (2001). *Inner Peace for Busy People: 52 Simple Strategies for Transforming Your Life*. Carlsbad: Hay House. Suggestions for inner balance.

Carlson, R., & Bailey, J. (1997). *Slowing Down to the Speed of Life: How To Create A More Peaceful, Simpler Life From the Inside Out*. New York: HarperCollins. Find calm and sanity by changing your attitude, not by downsizing your life.

Dyer, W. (2004). *The Power of Intention: Learning to Co-Create Your World Your Way*. Hay House. How positive intentions create positive outcomes.

Easwaran, E. (1992). *Your Life Is Your Message: Finding Harmony With Yourself, Others & the Earth*. New York: Hyperion. How making small daily changes in the way we think and live can change our world.

Glanz, B. (2003). *Balancing Acts - More Than 250 Guiltfree, Creative Ideas to Blend Your Work & Your Life*. Dearborn Trade Publishing. Strategies for blending life's roles.

Honore, C. (2004). *In Praise of Slow: How a Worldwide Movement Is Challenging the Cult of Speed*. Toronto: Random House. Exploring our driven relationship with time.

Irvine, D. (1997). *Simple Living in a Complex World: Balancing Life's Achievements*. Calgary: Redstone Publishing. Practical exercises for building a successful l life.

Kabat-Zinn, J. (2005). *Coming to Our Senses: Healing Ourselves and the World Through Mindfulness*. New York: Hyperion. A passionate tour de force that blends personal experience with cutting-edge science.

Kavelin Popov, L. (2004). *A Pace of Grace: The Virtues of a Sustainable Life*. New York: Penguin. Practices for living a meaningful life in balance and wellness.

Kundtz, D. (2003). *Quiet Mind: One-Minute Retreats from a Busy World*. Berkley: Connari Press. Thoughtful insights for keeping life in perspective.

Laroche, L. (2003). *Life Is Short, Wear Your Party Pants.* Carlsbad: Hay House. Lighthearted ways to lighten up and overcome stress.

Levey, J., & Levey, M. (1998). ***Living in Balance: A Dynamic Approach for Creating Harmony & Wholeness in a Chaotic World***. Berkley: Connari Press. Finding harmony in love, work, eating, sleeping, exercise, and even breathing.

Loehr, J., & Schwartz, T. (2003). ***The Power of Full Engagement: Managing Energy, Not Time, is the Key to High Performance and Personal Renewal***. New York: Simon & Schuster. Managing energy as the key to high performance and personal renewal.

LoVerde, M. (1998). ***Stop Screaming at the Microwave: How to Connect Your Disconnected Life***. New York: Simon & Schuster. Offers inspiring ideas for reconnecting with self and others.

McGee-Cooper, A. (1990). ***You Don't Have to Go Home from Work Exhausted!: A Program to Bring Joy, Energy, and Balance to Your Life***. Bowen and Rogers. How to add energy enhancers and rejuvenators to every day of your life.

Menzies, H. (2005). ***No Time: Stress and the Crisis of Modern Life***. Vancouver: Douglas & McIntyre. A behind-the-scenes look at the drivers and impact of a culture spinning out of control.

Muller, W. (1999). ***Sabbath: Finding Rest, Renewal, and Delight in Our Busy Lives***. New York: Bantam Books. Presents a convincing historical case and present-day argument for building pauses into our lives on a regular basis.

Nerburn, K. (1998). ***Small Graces: The Quiet Gifts of Everyday Life***. Novato, CA: New World Library. An insightful commentary that encourages us to find meaning in everyday experiences.

Percy, I. (1999). ***Going Deep: Exploring Spirituality in Life and Leadership***. Blue Hill: Medicine Bear Publishing. A guide to making work meaningful.

Posen, D. M.D. (2003). ***The Little Book of Stress Relief***. Toronto: Key Porter Books. A doctor's 52 prescriptions for a calmer life.

St James, E. (2001). ***Simplify Your Work Life: Ways to Change the Way You Work So You Have More Time to Live***. New York: Hyperion. Simplifying life on the job and scaling down the world of work.

Swenson, R. A. (1992). ***Margin: How to Create the Emotional, Physical, Financial and Time Reserves You Need***. Colorado Springs: Navpress. Re-establishing margin in our lives - that leeway that once existed between the loads we carry and our limits.

Zelinski, E. (1991). ***The Joy of Not Working***. Edmonton: Visions International Publishing. Bringing balance to life by putting work in perspective.

Zoglio, S. (2003). ***Recharge in Minutes: The Quick-Lift Way to Less Stress, More Success, and Renewed Energy***. Doylestown: Tower Hill Press. 101 ways to refuel.

Product Order Form

For detailed descriptions, see www.pauseworks.com or www.patkatz.com

____ # Press Pause ... Press On @ 19.95 = _____

____ # Give Me A Break Booklets @ $6.95 = _____

____ # Expert Women Who Speak ... Speak Out @ $19.95 = _____

____ # WorkTips @ $14.95 = _____

____ # HomeTips @ $14.95 = _____

Handling & Postage

Books	Booklets
$3 for 1	$1 for 1
$6 for 2-5	$2 for 2-5
$12 for 6-15	$5 for 6-20
$15 for 16+	$10 for 21-49

Handling & Postage = _____

Subtotal = _____

Canadian Orders add 6% GST = _____

Total Amount of Order = _____

(U.S. & international orders payable in U.S. funds)

☐ Check or money order payable to Optimus Consulting
☐ VISA   ☐ MCard   ☐ Amex

Cardholder Name: _____

Card#: _____ Expiry Date: _____

Name: _____ Ph: _____

Street: _____

City: _____ Province/State: _____ Code: _____

Mail your order to:
Optimus Consulting, 315 O'Brien Place, Saskatoon SK, S7K 6S9

Fax your order to - (306) 242-0795   Call toll free to - (877) 728-5289

Shop online at - www.pauseworks.com or www.patkatz.com

For fund-raising or volume purchases:
Contact Patricia Katz at Optimus Consulting for further information
Phone toll free - (877) 728-5289.